THIS WORLD: PLAYGROUND OR BATTLEGROUND?

This
WORLD:
PLAYGROUND
or
BATTLEGROUND?

A.W. TOZER

CHOSEN AND EDITED BY
HARRY VERPLOEGH

CHRISTIAN PUBLICATIONS, INC.
CAMP HILL, PENNSYLVANIA

Christian Publications, Inc.
3825 Hartzdale Drive, Camp Hill, PA 17011
www.cpi-horizon.com
www.christianpublications.com

Faithful, biblical publishing since 1883

ISBN: 0-87509-420-1
LOC Catalog Card Number: 88-93033
© 1988 by Christian Publications

CONTENTS

PUBLISHER'S FOREWORD

I FIRST HEARD A.W. TOZER on July 4, 1946, at Delta Lake Bible Conference Center in Rome, New York. He preached from Colossians 1:15-17 on the supremacy of Jesus Christ. As a young ex-serviceman, I sat spellbound as that master pulpiteer exalted our Savior and Lord in a remarkable message. Now, forty-two years later, I have had the twin honor of being one of his successors as editor of *Alliance Life*, the official magazine of The Christian and Missionary Alliance, and more recently, of being the publisher of most of his books.

Since the first copies of *The Pursuit of God* rolled from the presses of Christian Publications, people who bought Tozer's work instinctively knew they had discovered a twentieth century prophet. For the thirteen years that Dr. Tozer edited *Alliance Life*, this self-taught, Spirit-taught Pennsylvanian produced a veritable gold mine of editorials. People subscribed to the magazine just to read his incisive writing. Occasionally, of course, Tozer referred to then-current issues or events, such as the Korean War. Strike those dated sentences, and it is amazing how contemporary his editorials are after thirty-five or more years. Such is the mark of a true prophet.

Over the years many of those editorials have been preserved in books, the first three of which were prepared by Dr. Tozer himself. Then Anita Bailey, his managing editor, produced the next three collections after his death. In 1984 Harry Verploegh, a retired Chicago businessman who sat for thirty years under the preaching of Dr. Tozer and who became his friend and confidant, undertook to arrange the remaining material for publication. *This World: Playground or Battleground?* is the tenth book of Tozer editorials and the fourth that Verploegh has chosen and edited. Four more are in the plans, and then the project will be complete.

If this is your first introduction to the writings of A.W. Tozer, you are about to have your mind stimulated and your heart warmed. Plunge in at once! Join the large company of readers who continue to be drawn to one who through the media of pulpit and print shared with fellow believers his knowledge of the Holy.

H. Robert Cowles
Executive Vice-President
Christian Publications
December 1988

This World: Playground or Battleground?

Things are for us not only what they are—they are what we hold them to be. That is to say, our attitude toward things is likely in the long run to be more important than the things themselves. This is a common coin of knowledge, like an old dime worn smooth by use, yet it bears upon it the stamp of truth and must not be rejected simply because it is familiar.

It is strange how a fact may remain fixed, while our interpretation of the fact changes with the generations and the years. One such fact is the world in which we live. It is here and has been here through the centuries. It is a stable fact, quite unchanged by the passage of time, but how different is modern man's view of it from the view our fathers held! Here we see plainly how great is the power of interpretation. The world is for all of us not only what it is—it is what we believe it to be. And a tremendous load of woe or weal rides on the soundness of our interpretation.

Going back no further than the times of the founding and early development of our country, we are able to see the wide gulf between our modern attitudes and those of our fathers. In the early days, when Christianity exercised a dominant influence over American thinking, men conceived the world to be a battleground. Our fathers believed in sin and the devil and hell as constituting one force, and they believed in God and righteousness and heaven as the other. By their very nature, these forces were opposed to each other forever in deep, grave, irreconcilable hostility. Man, our fathers held, had to choose sides—he could not be neutral. For him it must be life or death, heaven or hell, and if he chose to come out on God's side, he could expect open war with God's enemies. The fight would be real and deadly and would last as long as life continued here below. Men looked forward to heaven as a return from the wars, a laying down of the sword to enjoy in peace the home prepared for them.

Sermons and songs in those days often had a martial quality about them, or perhaps a trace of homesickness. The Christian soldier thought of home and rest and reunion, and his voice grew plaintive as he sang of battle ended and victory won. But whether he was charging into enemy guns or dreaming of war's end and the Father's welcome home, he never forgot what kind of world he lived in—it was a battleground, and many were wounded and slain.

That view is unquestionably scriptural. Allowing for the figures and metaphors with which the Scriptures abound, it is still a solid Bible doctrine that tremendous spiritual forces are present in the world. Man, because of his spiritual nature, is caught in the middle. The evil powers are bent upon destroying him, while Christ is present to save him through the power of the gospel. To obtain deliverance he must come out on God's side in faith and obedience. That in brief is what our fathers thought, and that, we believe, is what the Bible teaches.

How different today. The fact remains the same, but the interpretation has changed completely. Men think of the world not as a battleground, but as a playground. We are not here to fight; we are here to frolic. We are not in a foreign land; we are at home. We are not getting ready to live, but we are already living, and the best we can do is rid ourselves of our inhibitions and our frustrations and live this life to the full. This, we believe, is a fair summary of the religious philosophy of modern man, openly professed by millions and tacitly held by many more millions who live out that philosophy without having given it verbal expression.

This changed attitude toward the world has had and is having its effect upon Christians, even gospel Christians who profess the faith of the Bible. By a curious juggling of the figures, they manage to add up the column wrong and yet claim to have the right answer. It sounds fantastic, but it is true.

The idea that this world is a playground instead of a battleground has now been accepted in practice by the vast majority of fundamentalist Christians. They might hedge around the question if they were asked bluntly to declare their position, but their conduct gives them away. They are facing both ways, enjoying Christ *and* the world, gleefully telling everyone that accepting Jesus does not require them to give up their fun—Christianity is just the jolliest thing imaginable. The "worship" growing out of such a view of life is as far off center as the view itself—a sort of sanctified nightclub without the champagne and the dressed-up drunks.

This whole thing has grown to be so serious that it is now the bound duty of all Christians to reexamine their spiritual philosophy in the light of the Bible. Having discovered the scriptural way, they must follow it, even if to do so, they must separate themselves from much that they had accepted as real, but which now in the light of truth is seen to be false.

A right view of God and the world to come requires that we have a right view of the world in which we live and of our relationship to it. So much depends upon this that we cannot afford to be careless about it.

A Scared World Needs a Fearless Church

No one can blame people for being afraid. The world is in for a baptism of fire, and whether or not this present conflict is the beginning of the ordeal, such a baptism will surely come sooner or later. God declares this by the voice of all the holy prophets since time began—there is no escaping it.

But are not we Christians a people of another order? Do we not claim a place in the purpose of God altogether above the uncertainties of time and chance in which the sons of this world are caught? Have we not been given a prophetic preview off all those things that are to come upon the earth? Can anything take us unaware?

Surely Bible-reading Christians should be the last persons on earth to give way to hysteria. They are redeemed from their past offenses, kept in their present circumstances by the power of an all-powerful God, and their future is safe in His hands. God has promised to support them in the flood, protect them in the fire, feed them in famine, shield them against their enemies, hide them in His safe chambers until the indignation is past and receive them at last into eternal tabernacles.

If we are called upon to suffer, we may be perfectly sure that we shall be rewarded for every pain and blessed for every tear. Underneath will be the Everlasting Arms and within will be the deep assurance that all is well with our souls. Nothing can separate us from the love of God—not death, nor life, nor height, nor depth, nor any other creature.

This is a big old world, and it is full of the habitations of darkness, but nowhere in its vast expanse is there one thing of which a real Christian need be afraid. Surely a fear-ridden Christian has never examined his or her defenses.

A fear-stricken church cannot help a scared world. We who are in the secret place of safety must begin to talk and act like it. We, above all who dwell upon the earth, should be calm, hopeful, buoyant and cheerful. We'll never convince the scared world that there is peace at the Cross if we continue to exhibit the same fears as those who make no profession of Christianity.

We Face Tomorrow
without Fear

Every new year is an uncharted and unknown sea. No ship has ever sailed this way before. The wisest of earth's sons and daughters cannot tell us what we may encounter on this journey. Familarity with the past may afford us a general idea of what we may expect, but just where the rocks lie hidden beneath the surface or when that "tempestuous wind called Euroclydon" may sweep down upon us suddenly, no one can say with certainty.

Conditions over the world are so grave that no one who thinks at all is able any longer to maintain a spirit of optimism. The world's philosophers have long ago ceased to preach peace, except as a goal toward which the nations should frantically struggle even while they have but little hope of attaining it.

The best brains of the world have gone into the production of tools with which to destroy the world. And if they do such things in the green tree, what shall they do in the dry?

When Pharaoh was faced with trouble, he sent for Joseph; Nebuchadnezzar in distress called upon Daniel. These enlightened men of God knew the score—they could predict the future and point the way to safety. They were wise with a wisdom not of this world and so were able to face the future with cheerfulness even when they knew how dark and troubled that future would be.

Today also there are a few men and women who can face the coming year without discouragement or terror. They are Christians. They are not smiling optimists who draw their comfort from a denial of the facts or base their hopes upon false expectations of peaceful intentions among nations. Rather, they are of all men the truest realists. They will have nothing to do with fantasy—they demand to know the facts, whether those facts are good or bad. They insist upon squaring their beliefs with the truth, and do not hesitate to face up to any truth wherever it is found.

Now more than at any other time in generations, the believer is in a position to go on the offensive. The world is lost on a wide sea, and the Christian alone knows the way to the desired haven. While things were going well, the world scorned him with his Bible and his hymns, but now they need him desperately, and they need that despised Bible, too. For in the Bible, and there only, is found the chart to tell us where we are on this rough and unknown ocean. The day when the Christian should meekly apologize is over—he can get the world's attention not by trying to please, but by boldly declaring the truth of divine revelation. He can make himself heard not by compromise, but by taking the affirmative and sturdily declaring, "Thus saith the LORD" (Exodus 4:22).

Whatever the world does in the years ahead, and whatever happens among mankind, true Christians have no cause for worry. They are safe forever by a covenant of blood and are dearer to God than the apple of His eye. No night can be dark enough to put out their light, no fire hot enough to burn them, no flood severe enough to drown them on their journey. The winds and waves are their friends and the stars in their courses fight for them. God is at their right hand, and they shall not be moved.

Let us then face tomorrow with praise and song; let us live in a state of perpetual worship. For are we not kept by the power of God "unto salvation ready to be revealed in the last time" (1 Peter 1:5)? And the "last time" may be nearer than we think.

We Must Have True Faith

To many Christians, Christ is little more than an idea, or at best an ideal—He is not a fact. Millions of professed believers talk as if He were real and act as if He were not. Our actual position is always to be discovered by the way we act, not by the way we talk.

We can prove our faith by our commitment to it and in no other way. Any belief that does not command the one who holds it is not a real belief—it is only a pseudo-belief. It might shock some of us profoundly if we were suddenly brought face-to-face with our beliefs and forced to test them in the fires of practical living.

Many of us have become extremely skillful in arranging our lives so as to admit the truth of Christianity without being embarrassed by its implications. We fix things so that we can get on well enough without divine aid, while at the same time ostensibly seeking it. We boast in the Lord but carefully watch that we never get caught depending on Him. "The heart is deceitful above all things, and desperately wicked: who can know it?" (Jeremiah 17:9).

Pseudo-faith always arranges a way out in case God fails. Real faith knows only one way and gladly allows itself to be stripped of any second ways or makeshift substitutes. For true faith, it is either God or total collapse. And since Adam first stood up on the earth, God has not failed a single man or woman who trusted Him.

Those of pseudo-faith will fight for their verbal creed but flatly refuse to allow themselves to get into a predicament where their future depends upon that creed being true. They always provide themselves with secondary ways of escape so they will have a way out if the roof caves in.

What we need these days is a company of Christians who are prepared to trust God as completely now as they know they must at the last day. For each of us the time is surely coming when we shall have nothing but God. Health and wealth and friends and hiding places will all be swept away and we shall have only God. To those of pseudo-faith that is a terrifying thought, but to real faith it is one of the most comforting thoughts the heart can entertain.

It would be tragedy indeed to come to the place where we have nothing but God and find that we had not been trusting God at all during the days of our earthly sojourn. It would be better to *invite*

God now to remove every false trust, to disengage our hearts from all secret hiding places and to bring us out into the open where we can discover for ourselves whether or not we really trust Him. That is a harsh cure for our troubles, but it is a sure one. Gentler cures may be too weak to do the work, and time is running out on us.

"When All Thy Mercies, O My God"

Not many of the literary great have attained to prominence in the Church of the First-born. There have, however, been a view exceptions. Among those we would put John Milton, George Herbert and Joseph Addison.

Among the gems left us by Addison is a Thanksgiving hymn, *When All Thy Mercies, O My God*. This hymn appears in the better hymnals and is sung wherever men love to bring exquisite poetry to the service of praise.

> When all Thy mercies, O my God
>   My rising soul surveys,
> Transported with the view, I'm lost
>   In wonder, love and praise.

The figure of the mercies of God lying outspread like a vast and variegated landscape is beautiful enough in itself, and when we add to it the picture of the soul rising as from guilty sleep to look out in wonder over the boundless expanse, when we see that soul suddenly rapt into transports of delight with everything it sees until it finally sinks down in a kind of delightful swoon, "lost in wonder, love and praise," we have a mental image that requires music to express.

Again he sings,

> Ten thousand thousand precious gifts
>   My daily thanks employ;
> Nor is the least a cheerful heart
>   That tastes these gifts with joy.

Here is the true spirit of Thanksgiving. Here is understanding of what pleases God in our acceptance and use of His gifts. "A cheerful heart that tastes these gifts with joy" is the only kind of heart that can taste those gifts safely. There is the idea expressed elsewhere on these pages that our indebtedness to God is so great that nothing less than "daily thanks" will be enough to satisfy our hearts or please the heart of God.

While Addison had in mind chiefly the gifts that God showers upon us here below, he was too much of a Christian to think that God's gifts or his own praise would cease at death. So he sang,

> Through every period of my life
>   Thy goodness I'll pursue;
> And after death, in distant worlds,
>   The glorious theme renew.

It is quite in keeping with such a spirit that the poet should call his son-in-law to his side at the last and whisper, "See in what peace a Christian can die."

On Wrestling in Prayer

There is an idea abroad that wrestling in prayer is always a good thing, but that is by no means true. Extreme religious exercises may be undergone with no higher motive than to get our own way.

The spiritual quality of a prayer is determined not by its intensity but by its origin. In evaluating prayer we should inquire who is doing the praying—our determined hearts or the Holy Spirit? If the prayer originates with the Holy Spirit, then the wrestling can be beautiful and wonderful; but if we are the victims of our own overheated desires, our praying can be as carnal as any other act.

Two examples are given in the Old Testament, Jacob and the prophets of Baal. Jacob's wrestling was a real exercise, and at first it was not Jacob's doing. "And Jacob was left alone; and there wrestled a man with him until the breaking of the day" (Genesis 32:24). Obviously the "man" was the aggressor, not Jacob, but when Jacob had been beaten upon, he became the aggressor and cried, "I will not let thee go, except thou bless me" (32:26). The wrestling was of divine origin, and the blessed results are known to every Bible student.

The other example does not turn out so well. The prophets of Baal wrestled also, much more violently that Jacob, but they wrestled in the flesh. Their writhings were born of ignorance and superstition and got them nowhere. Everything was a mistake—their zeal, their body-punishing prayer, their determination. They were wrong in spite of their zealous praying. And such error did not die with them.

Only the Spirit can pray effectively. "Likewise the Spirit also helpeth our infirmities: for we know not what we should pray for as we ought: but the Spirit itself maketh intercession for us with groanings which cannot be uttered" (Romans 8:26).

Men, Our Most Critical Need

The most critical need of the Church at this moment is men—the right kind of men, bold men. The talk is that we need revival, that we need a new baptism of the Holy Spirit—and God knows we must have both—but God will not revive mice. He will not fill rabbits with the Holy Spirit.

We languish for men who feel themselves expendable in the warfare of the soul because they have already died to the allurements of this world. Such men will be free from the compulsions that control weaker men. They will not be forced to do things by the squeeze of circumstances. Their only compulsion will come from within—or from above.

This kind of freedom is necessary if we are to have prophets in our pulpits again instead of mascots. These free men will serve God and mankind from motives too high to be understood by the rank and file of religious retainers who today shuttle in

and out of the sanctuary. They will make no deci-
sions out of fear, take no course out of a desire to
please, accept no service for financial considerations, perform no religious acts out of mere custom, nor allow themselves to be influenced by the
love of publicity or the desire for reputation.

Much that the church—even the evangelical
church—is doing today, it is doing because it is
afraid not to do it. Ministerial associations take up
projects for no higher reasons than that they are
scared into it. Whatever their ear-to-the-ground,
fear-inspired reconnoitering leads them to believe—or fear—the world expects them to do,
they will be doing come next Monday morning
with all kinds of trumped-up zeal and show of
godliness. The pressure of public opinion calls
these prophets, not the voice of Jehovah.

The true church has never sounded out public
expectations before launching its crusades. Its leaders heard from God and went ahead wholly inde-
pendent of popular support or the lack of it. They
knew their Lord's will and did it, and their people
followed them—sometimes to triumph, but more
often to insults and public persecution—and their
sufficient reward was the satisfaction of being right
in a wrong world.

Another characteristic of the true prophet has
been love. The free man who has learned to hear
God's voice and dared to obey it has felt the moral
burden that broke the hearts of the Old Testament
prophets, crushed the soul of our Lord Jesus Christ,

and wrung streams of tears from the eyes of the apostles.

The free man has never been a religious tyrant, nor has he sought to lord it over God's heritage. It is fear and lack of self-assurance that has led men to try to bring others under their feet. They have had some interest to protect, some position to secure, so they have demanded subjection from their followers as a guarantee of their own safety. But the free man—never. He has nothing to protect, no ambition to pursue and no enemy to fear. For that reason he is completely careless of his standing among men. If they follow him—well and good. If not, he loses nothing that he holds dear. But whether he is accepted or rejected, he will go on loving his people with sincere devotion, and only death can silence his tender intercession for them.

Yes, if evangelical Christianity is to stay alive, it must have men again—the right kind of men. It must repudiate the weaklings who dare not speak out, and it must seek in prayer and much humility the coming again of men of the stuff of which prophets and martyrs are made. God will hear the cries of His people as He heard the cries of Israel in Egypt, and He will send deliverance by sending deliverers. It is His way.

And when the deliverers come—reformers, revivalists, prophets—they will be men of God and men of courage. They will have God on their side because they are careful to stay on God's side. They will be coworkers with Christ and instruments in the hands of the Holy Spirit. Such men will be baptized with the Spirit indeed and through their labors He will baptize others and send the long-delayed revival.

The Spiritual Person

Almost every Christian wants to be spiritual, but few know what the experience means. A lot of unfounded comfort could be swept away and much true consolation received if we could get straightened out.

It is difficult for us to shake off the notion that a person is as spiritual as he or she feels. Our basic spirituality seldom accords our feelings. There are many carnal persons whose religious emotions are sensitive to every impression and who manage to keep themselves on a fairly high plane of inward enjoyment but who have no marks of godliness upon them. They have a low boiling point and can get heated up over almost anything religious at a moment's notice. Their tears are close to the surface and their voices carry a world of emotional content. Such have a reputation for being spiritual, and they themselves may easily believe they are. But they are not necessarily so.

Spiritual people are indifferent to their feelings— they live by faith in God with little care about their own emotions. They think God's thoughts and see things as God sees them. They rejoice in Christ and have no confidence in themselves. They are more concerned with obedience than with happiness. This is less romantic, perhaps, but it will stand the test of fire.

Our Resources for the Years to Come

The custom of dividing time into years is of course altogether arbitrary and even a bit awkward. It requires a clear mind to remember that time is no servant of the calendar and that years do not come in neat packages like corn flakes. Nor do they come in nicely finished sections like a string of frankfurters.

In one sense a new year begins whenever we decide it shall. The various peoples of the world have not been in full agreement about their year's end and its new beginning, but we can start a new year whenever we purpose to rearrange our lives morally and invite Christ to become our Lord and Savior. At that moment we become new creatures—a "new name is written down in glory" and our new year begins. That moral rearrangement we call repentance, and the act of making a new creature we call regeneration. The soul that has experienced such a wondrous transformation is likely to place more emphasis upon that new start than he or she does upon our official New Year's Day.

As Christians we look at everything differently. The world knows what it trusts and what it wants—it knows its treasures and what constitutes them; it knows what it must have to make it happy and successful during the year ahead. Christians feel altogether different about the whole thing, and in doing so they are not simply being contrary—they are following the sure wisdom of the kingdom of God. They know they are sons and daughters of eternity and are not dependent upon the things of time.

People of the world, for instance, hope for life, health, financial prosperity, international peace and a set of favorable circumstances. These are their resources—upon them they rest. They look to them as a child looks to its nursing mother.

Christians do not despise these temporal blessings, and if they come to them, they sanctify them by receiving them with prayers of outpoured gratitude to God. But they know their everlasting welfare is not dependent upon them. These blessings may come or go, but true Christians abide in God where no evil can touch them and where they are rich beyond all the power of their minds to conceive—and this altogether apart from earthly circumstances.

Christians hope for peace, but if war comes it cannot rob them of anything essential to their eternal welfare. They hope for peace but are prepared to lay down their lives if they must, for the sake of righteousness. They hope for financial success, but if it passes them by, they have learned to be content with such things as they have. They hope that the world will be kind to them, but if it is not, they will not get panicky, because they remember the words spoken by our Lord, "In the world ye shall have tribulation: but be of good cheer; I have overcome the world" (John 16:33).

The world's resources are good in their way, but they have this fatal defect—they are uncertain and transitory. Today we have them, tomorrow they are gone. It is this way with all earthly things since sin came to upset the beautiful order of nature and made the human race victims of chance and change.

We desire for all of God's children a full measure of every safe and pure blessing which the earth and the sky might unite to bring them. But if in the sovereign will of God things go against us, what do we have left? If war overflows her banks in blood, if persecutions come, if life and health are placed in jeopardy, what about our everlasting resources?

If the world's foundations crumble we still have God, and in Him we have everything essential to our ransomed beings forever. We have Christ, who also died for us and who now sits at the right hand of the Majesty in the heavens making constant and effective intercession for us. We have the Scriptures, which can never fail. We have the Holy Spirit to interpret the Scriptures to our inner lives and to be to us a Guide and a Comforter. We have prayer and we have faith, and these bring heaven to earth and turn even bitter Marah sweet. And if worse comes to worst here below, we have our Father's house and our Father's welcome.

Let's Stay by the Scriptures

One school of Christian thought divides the grace of God into two kinds: "covenanted grace" and "uncovenanted grace"—the first being the grace of God as it operates through the gospel, and the second being the grace of God as it may operate sovereignly outside of and apart from the covenants of the Word. Uncovenanted grace would be that by which God met and blessed men and women before the covenants of Scripture were brought into being. It might also explain how God has enlightened human consciences and drawn us to the love of goodness even where the Word of God has not been preached.

This is a fascinating bit of side doctrine—and there seems to be no way to prove or disprove it—but it would be sheer folly to place any confidence in it. If God could operate satisfactorily outside His sacred covenants as revealed in the

Scriptures, it is hard to understand why He should go to such pains to make His great spiritual compacts with mankind and to cause them to be written down in the Word of truth for our enlightenment.

No, there is only one true source of light concerning the grace of God—the sacred Scriptures. Whatever God may say or be saying to the conscience of mankind, He speaks redemptively by the prophets and apostles, and by them alone. All authentic testimony about salvation centers around the cross of Christ and sounds forth from it to the whole world.

CHAPTER

11

A New Look at
an Old Question

The propensity to accept any current religious emphasis as the correct and only scriptural view runs deep in our nature, for it is simply the old love for status quo common to all peoples in every field of human thought. An idea is handed to us by those we respect; we check the references, accept the idea, find the whole thing mentally comfortable and proceed at once to identify it with orthodoxy. After that we judge people by the test of whether or not they subscribe to it. Naturally we resist any suggestion that perhaps the idea may need a bit of editing to bring it into line with the Scriptures and the historic faith of Christians.

The assertion that the eschatology of the past hundred years (held now by most fundamentalists) does not agree in every detail with the beliefs of the church fathers will be condemned as rank heresy by many present-day Christians. But the facts are easy to check—those who will take the trouble to read and study for themselves can do it.

The usual way of explaining the discrepancy, where such a discrepancy is known, is to assert sweepingly that those great Christians of the past who did not hold our views on prophecy were simply unenlightened. They were good Christians, to be sure, but they just never managed to rise to our height of prophetic vision. The Wesleys, for instance, and such men as Edwards, Knox and Rutherford, were fine as far as they went, but they were sadly lacking in the knowledge of end-time truth.

Apart from the fact that the same argument is advanced by the Jehovah's Witnesses and the Seventh-day Adventists to justify their views, there is at least one other reason for rejecting this too-neat way of explaining things—it puts us in the painful position of having to claim superiority over persons whom all the world knows were infinitely beyond us in every quality that goes to make spiritual greatness. Without wanting to be thought flippant, we might say that if Augustine and Bernard and Watts and Andrewes (English theologian, 1555-1626) became such flaming saints while yet blind to the truth of prophecy, and if modern fundamentalists are the kind of Christians *they* are while at the same time blessed with all prophetic knowledge, then sure it pays to be ignorant!

Christ will return to earth to wake the sleeping saints and glorify His faithful ones who are alive at His coming. We believe that His return is the hope of the church, hope that alone makes life on earth tolerable for us. But is it incompatible with that belief to desire to know what God has revealed about the future rather than to accept blindly what some school of prophetic thought would force upon us? Is it unspiritual to long for truth rather than to follow without examination eschatological teachings that were unknown to the saints of past times? We believe it is neither incompatible nor unspiritual.

The time has come for the ministry of teachers who will reexamine the whole prophetic question in the light of the Scriptures, who will not be awed by the big names of the last half century, but who will check the teachings of recent times against the beliefs of the great Christians of the past and allow those beliefs at least as much weight as the beliefs of modern teachers. We need some courageous people who can speak with spiritual authority, not those who are content merely to parrot the views of a few prophecy experts who have arrived at their present convictions by reading each other's books.

Perhaps, after all, the greatest prophetic problem facing us is one of readiness rather than one of knowledge. We may not always be sure we have every detail right, but we need never be uncertain about our moral and spiritual preparation for the great day of our Lord's coming. "Be ye also patient; stablish your hearts: for the coming of the Lord draweth nigh" (James 5:8).

Books and Moral Standards

The late Jimmy Walker, playboy mayor of New York during the roaring '20s, was widely quoted for a quip viewed as the distilled essence of gospel truth by those who wanted to believe it. "I never heard," said Jimmy, "of anyone who was ruined by a book."

These profound words were tossed off, as near as we can remember, during an official inquiry into the effect of certain questionable literature upon the morals of the reading public. Now, we can offer no proof that Mr. Walker had ever heard of anyone who had been ruined by a book, but that could only mean that the gentleman's knowledge on the subject was vastly small or that his idea of what it meant to be "ruined" was not the same as that of the more conscientious persons within our population who still feel bothered about the effect of bad reading upon the collective public mind. Whatever the explanation, Mr. Walker's implication that no one had ever been ruined by a bad book is 100 percent false. The facts are against it.

History will show that bad books have ruined not only individuals but whole nations as well. What the writings of Voltaire and Rousseau did to France is too well-known to need further mention here. Again, it would not be difficult to establish a cause and effect relationship between the philosophy of Friedrich Nietzsche and the bloody career of Adolph Hitler. Certainly the doctrines of Nietzsche appeared again in the mouthings of der Fuhrer and soon became the official party line for Nazi propagandists. And it is hardly conceivable that Russian communism could have come into being apart from the writings of Karl Marx.

The truth is that thoughts are things and words are seeds. The printed word may lie unnoticed like a seed through a long winter, only to burst out when a favorable time comes and produce an abundant crop in belief and practice. Many who are today useful members of the church were brought to Christ by the reading of a book. Thousands have witnessed to the power of the lowly gospel tract to capture the mind and focus the attention on God and on salvation.

Just what part evil literature has played in this present moral breakdown throughout our land will never be known till men are called forth to answer to a holy God for their unholy deeds. For thousands of young people, the first doubt about God and the Bible came with the reading of some evil book. We must respect the power of ideas. Printed ideas are as powerful as spoken ones—they may have a longer fuse, but their explosive power is just as great.

What all this adds up to is that we Christians are bound in all conscience to discourage the reading of subversive literature and to promote as fully as possible the circulation of good books and magazines. Our Christian faith teaches us to expect to answer for every idle word—how much more severely shall we be held to account for every evil word, whether printed or spoken.

Tolerance of noxious literature is not a mark of intellectual size—it may be a mark of secret sympathy for evil. Every book should stand or fall on its own merit, altogether apart from the reputation of its author. The fact that a nasty or suggestive book was written by an "accepted" writer does not make it less harmful. If it is bad, it is bad, regardless of its origin. Christians should judge a book by its purity, not by the reputation of the author.

The desire to appear broad-minded is not easy to overcome, because it is rooted in our ego and is simply a none-too-subtle form of pride. In the name of broad-mindedness many a Christian home has been opened to literature that sprang not from a broad mind but from a little mind, dirty and polluted with evil.

We require our children to wipe their feet before entering the house. Dare we demand less of the literature that comes into our home?

CHAPTER

13

On Getting Smaller Trying to Get Big

Some time ago we heard a short address by a young preacher during which he quoted the following, "If you are too big for a little place, you are too little for a big place."

It is an odd rule of the kingdom of God that when we try to get big, we always get smaller by the moment. God is jealous of His glory and will not allow any man to share it with Him. The effort to appear great among men will bring the displeasure of God upon us and effectively prevent us from achieving the greatness after which we pant.

Humility pleases God wherever it is found, and the humble man will have God for his friend and helper always. Only the humble man is completely sane, for he is the only one who sees clearly his own size and limitations. The egotist sees things out of focus. To himself he is large and God is correspondingly small, and that is a kind of moral insanity. Humility is a coming back to sanity like Nebuchadnezzar. The humble man evaluates everything correctly, and that makes him a wise man and a philosopher.

Young Christians often hinder their own usefulness by their attitude toward themselves. They begin with the innocent notion that they are at least a bit above the average in intelligence and ability, and consequently they feel shy about taking a humble place. They want to begin at the top and work upward! What happens is that they usually fail to secure the high place they feel qualified to fill and end up developing a chronic feeling of resentment toward everyone who stands in their way or fails to appreciate them. And as they grow older that comes to include almost everybody. At last comes a deep permanent grudge against the world. They settle at last into a state of sour saintliness and develop a look of holy hurt they fancy must have been on the faces of the martyrs in the arena.

This is too serious to be funny and too tragically harmful to take lightly. The simple fact is that no one can stand in the way of a completely humbled man. There aren't enough mountains in hell to hold down the true man or woman of God even if they were piled on him or her at once. God chooses the meek to confound the mighty. "Out of the mouth of babes and sucklings hast thou ordained strength because of thine enemies, that thou mightest still the enemy and the avenger" (Psalm 8:2). Babies pass for just what they are—they have no pride in themselves and they bear no grudges. Here's a tip for Christians.

Imitative, Conservative or Creative—Which?

G od is creative. He has not relinquished His place as Creator, even though the specific work of forming the first heaven and earth has long been completed.

The Holy Spirit as one of the blessed Godhead is also creative. He is forever bringing new things into being, forever giving out and setting in motion, forever making "all things new." Wherever He is at work, the effects will be creative rather than conservative, though we should know that He also conserves whatever He creates. To create and not conserve would be to waste the creative act. But the whole psychology of the Spirit is toward the creation of new things rather than toward the cautious preservation of what has been created.

It should be said that the Holy Spirit always creates in accord with His character as very God of very God. He stamps whatever He does with the mark of eternity. It has upon it the quality of everlastingness—the dignity and holiness of the Deity set it apart.

When the Holy Spirit is ignored or rejected, religious people are forced either to do their own creating or to fossilize completely. A few churches accept fossilization as the will of God and settle down to the work of preserving their past—as if it needed preserving. Others seek to appear modern, and imitate the current activities of the world with the mistaken idea that they are being creative. And after a fashion they are, but the creatures of their creative skill are sure to be toys and trifles, mere imitations of the world and altogether lacking in the qualities of eternity—holiness and spiritual dignity. The hallmark of the Holy Spirit is not there.

All religious leaders should remember that they will either let the Holy Spirit work through them or their work will be in vain. Every proud religious edifice erected by the zeal and labor of the flesh will perish in the hot fires of judgment. In the eyes of humanity such labors may be praiseworthy, but before God the results will be wood, hay and stubble.

It is hard to imagine a more painful disillusionment than to come to the judgment seat of Christ and find that all our earthly lives we had been striving after the flesh and never permitting the creative Holy Spirit to work in us that which was pleasing in His sight.

So all Christians and all churches are engaged in one of three activities: guarding the dead past, creating fleshly trifles that will perish with the flesh or working in cooperation with the Holy Spirit in the constant creation of eternal treasures that will outlast the stars.

Motive is All-Important

T he big question at last will not be so much, "What did you do?" but "Why did you do it?" In moral acts, motive is everything. Of course it is important to do the right thing, but it is still more important to do the right thing for a right reason.

Intention is a large part of the action, whether done by good or bad people. The man who wills his enemy dead has, in the eyes of God, killed him already. "Whosoever looketh on a woman to lust after her hath committed adultery with her already in his heart" (Matthew 5:28). Not the overt act, but the will and the intention constitute the guilt.

Any act performed for an evil or selfish purpose is a bad act no matter how good it may in itself seem. Any act done out of love is a good act, even if through ignorance or failure the outcome is not found to be good for the one concerned. A Christian mother, for instance, who rises in the small hours of the morning to care for a sick child only because she loves him and wishes him well is performing a good act even if in her ignorance she may actually harm the child by failing to care for him properly. And the mother who would rise in cold anger to look after a child she hated would be performing a bad act even if her superior skill enabled her to care for him well.

We should carefully consider our motives. Some day soon they will be there to bless us or curse us. And from them there will be no appeal, for the Judge knows the thoughts and intents of the heart.

Something Beyond Song

There is a notion widely held among Christians that song is the highest possible expression of the joy of the Lord in the soul of a man. That idea is so near to being true that it may seem spiritually rude to challenge it. We have no wish to pick theological lint or pluck the wings off religious flies for the thrill such a sadistic act might afford. There are probably hundreds of wrong notions in all our heads, notions that, while they are wrong, are still too insignificant to deserve attention. They are like the minor physical blemishes we all have, harmless if not beautiful, and altogether too trivial to rate mention by serious-minded people.

The idea, however, that song is the supreme expression of any and all possible spiritual experience is not small; it is large and meaningful and needs to be brought to the test of the Scriptures and Christian testimony. Both the Bible and the testimony of a thousand saints show that there is experience beyond song. There are delights, which the heart may enjoy in the awesome Presence of God, that cannot find expression in language—they belong to the unutterable element in Christian experience. Not many enjoy them because not many know they can. The whole concept of ineffable worship has been lost to this generation of Christians. Our level of life is so low that no one expects to know the deep things of the soul until the Lord returns. So we are content to wait, and while we wait we are inclined to cheer our hearts sometimes by breaking into song.

Now, far be it from us to discourage the art of singing. Creation itself took its rise in a burst of song, Christ rose from the dead and sang among His brethren, and we are promised that they who dwell in dust will rise and sing at the resurrection. The Bible is a musical book and, next to Scriptures themselves, the best book to own is a good hymnbook. But there is still something beyond song.

The Bible and Christian biography emphasize silence, but today we use silence in exactly nothing. The average service in gospel circles these days is kept alive by noise. By making a religious din we assure our faltering hearts that everything is well. Conversely, we suspect silence and regard it as proof that the meeting is "dead." Even the most devout seem to think they must storm heaven with loud outcries and mighty bellowing or their prayers are of no avail.

Now, not all silence is spiritual. Some Christians are silent because they have nothing to say; others are silent because what they have to say cannot be uttered by mortal tongues. We will not speak of the first at the moment, but will confine our remarks to the latter.

Where the Holy Spirit is permitted to exercise His full sway in a redeemed heart, the progression is likely to be as follows: first, voluble praise, in speech or prayer or witness. Then, when the crescendo rises beyond the ability of studied speech to express, comes song. When song breaks down under the weight of glory, then comes silence where the soul, held in deep fascination, feels itself blessed with an unutterable beatitude.

At the risk of being written off as an extremist or a borderline fanatic, we offer it as our mature opinion that more spiritual progress can be made in one short moment of speechless silence in the awesome Presence of God than in years of mere study. While our mental powers are in command, there is always the veil of nature between us and the face of God. It is only when our vaunted wisdom has been met and defeated in a breathless encounter with Omniscience that we are permitted to really know. When prostrate and wordless, the soul receives divine knowledge like the flash of light on sensitive film. The exposure may be brief, but the results are permanent.

On the Misuse of Scripture

Of all the books in the world, the one most quoted, most misunderstood and most misapplied is the Bible. The error out of which this wide misuse of the Scripture springs is the notion that everything written in the Bible applies indiscriminately to everyone. This is a great mistake—no careful thinker should be deceived by it. God's Word is addressed only to certain persons—that is, those who stand in a special relationship toward Him under the terms of redemption. Just as the Gentile nations could not claim the covenant promises that God had made with Israel, so the assurances and promises made to repentant and believing persons cannot be applied to those who are neither believing nor penitent.

The sacred words of Jesus, "Greater love hath no man than this, that a man lay down his life for his friends," (John 15:13) have been applied to almost

47

everyone who has given his life in the line of duty—the policeman on the beat, the doctor who crawls into a mine to minister to an injured man or the soldier who dies on the field of battle. The words are used to sanctify the acts of many men who were anything but believers and who would laugh at the whole business if they were alive to know what was going on. Christ was talking about Himself and His approaching sacrifice on the cross. The context makes this clear, and when we apply the words otherwise, we do so on our own authority and at our own risk.

Adlai Stevenson, former governor of Illinois, when going through the throes of deciding whether or not he should let his name stand for nomination for the presidency, reportedly had a deep indisposition for the office. He was quoted as having repeated the words of Christ in the garden of Gethsemane, "O my Father, if it be possible, let this cup pass from me: nevertheless not as I will, but as thou wilt" (Matthew 26:39).

Now it is remotely possible that a true saint of God, in a moment of awful and heart-searching prayer, might in hushed reverence quote these words of the Savior and apply them to his or her own case. But their use at a political convention came as a dash of cold water in the face of some who heard. In the midst of endless billows of hoarse shouting, grandiose and unsupported claims of achievements, bitter and abusive denunciating of others who did not agree with them, senseless and moronic acts of childish demonstrating, "snake dancing" and horn blowing, obsequious flattering and downright lying, it is hard to see how the spirit of our Lord's solemn and tender words could have a place. All political conventions are alike, regardless of party, and should Christ appear at one of them and demand that His Lordship be acknowledged and His commandments be obeyed, He would be forthright shouted down and led from the room by the sergeant at arms. Yet His words are quoted as if they had a place there—surely a painful misapplication of Scripture.

We once knew a rather dissolute young man who, in spite of his loose living, prided himself on the number of Scriptures he could quote. One night in an ordeal of anguished repentance, he turned from all sin and sought salvation through Christ. His condition seemed hopeless, but he hung on with the desperation of faith. At last the light broke and he entered into life. Telling about it afterward, he admitted with a wry smile that in the hour of his agony every verse of Scripture he had known departed from him except one—"With men this is impossible; but with God all things are possible" (Matthew 19:26).

The Holy Spirit reserves the right to activate the truth in the souls of those who come to God in the meekness of humility, but a careless or irreverent use of the words of the Bible can do no good and may do irremediable harm.

Meditation among Falling Leaves

Here in the North, the fields are turning brown and the maples blaze red along country lanes and on village lawns everywhere. The air is faintly sweet with the incense of burning leaves as man and nature join together to celebrate the passing of summer and the coming of the "melancholy days" of which the good gray Bryant sang. The sky is a determined blue and the sun shines bravely, though its light is muted by the smoke from a thousand gentle fires fed by curled and faded garlands, which only a few days ago crowned the proud brows of the trees.

We may as well face it—Indian Summer is on us again and there will be frost any night now, or perhaps even the first experimental flakes of snow, deceptive harbingers of the deep and heavy drifts that will surely follow.

It is warm yet and the signs of summer have not all disappeared, but one thing is missing—the sound of bird song lately heard in town and country and sometimes even in the depths of the great cities. The woods are strangely silent now, where a few short weeks ago a thousand bird voices chorused the rising and setting of the sun.

Where are they, those rustic Carusos of the tree and bush, those Asaphs of the field and the hedgerow? Shame to tell, but they have gone from us just when we needed them most. They have fled to the south to escape the first breath of winter. They nested in our trees and fed in our grainfields while the summer was with us, but they forgot so soon, and they left us without so much as a friendly dip of a departing wing. And we are hurt a little, for we loved them well, and in spite of past experiences we trusted them, too. Nothing with so much melody in its throat could be faithless, so we thought, but we were wrong again—they have betrayed our confidence. They are gone, and while we are shivering beneath our turned-up coat collars they will be soaring over meadows alive with warmth and flowers and bright-hued insects.

Well, we can forgive them, for apparently nature made them to inhabit the sunshine; the frost kills their enthusiasm and destroys their song. They are summer friends, and we may as well accept them for what they are. But the flight of the summer birds can point up a moral for us if we are wise enough to see it, and the consideration of the birds might well make some of us uncomfortable. For there are

Christians that seem built for the sunshine only. They require a favorable temperature before they can act like Christians—they have never learned to carry their own climate with them. Those who manage to generate an unbelievable amount of enthusiasm while things are going well disappear at the first sign of trouble. They cannot serve God in the snow—they are strictly summer birds. They desert us at the approach of winter.

There can be no doubt that the cross was heavier for Christ to bear because of His disciples' actions—"And they all forsook him, and fled" (Mark 14:50). Paul knew the sick, sinking feeling that desertion brings when he wrote, "No man stood with me, but all men forsook me: I pray God that it may not be laid to their charge" (2 Timothy 4:16). Every true Christian, before he has lived long, will have occasion to understand in bitter experience these words of the apostle. Far too many religious persons are summer friends.

Now, what shall we do about these fickle friends? Pray for them and leave them with the Savior who died for them. He knows better than we do and to Him they will give account in the end. We dare not let them affect our spirits. We only note the fact of their existence and then pull on our overshoes and prepare to serve God in rough weather. When the spring comes, we'll be glad, but we refuse to run to escape the winter storms. We must be about our Father's business. He'll take care of the weather.

We Must Not
Defend, but Attack!

Too many of our religious convictions are negative. We act not from a positive conviction that something is right, but from a feeling that the opposite is wrong. We become allergic to certain beliefs and practice and react violently away from them. Thus our reactions become actions—we are driven to our positions by the enemy rather than led to them by the truth.

The faulty reasoning that leads to this is the assumption that if a man or woman is wrong on one thing, he or she is wrong on everything—if a liberal or a cultist is known to favor a belief, we shy away from the belief not because we know why it is wrong but because we know who holds it. We are thus always on the defensive. We back into our positions like stubborn horses rather than walking into them face forward like obedient sheep. The way to be right, so we reason, is to watch the enemy, discover what he favors, then choose the opposite.

That many of our hotly defended beliefs are no more than reactions to what we consider false doctrines would not be difficult to prove. The doctrine of justification by works (itself a serious error), for instance, has driven some teachers to espouse the equally damaging error of salvation without works. To many people the thought of "works" is repugnant because of its association with the effete Judaism of the New Testament era and the Catholicism of more recent times. The upshot of the matter is that we have salvation without righteousness and right doctrine without right deeds. Grace is twisted out of its moral context and made the cause of lowered standards of conduct in the church.

Again, the fear of "legalism" has driven some of God's good people to positions so grotesque as to be ridiculous. Some years ago, in a church paper, we came across an example of this negative kind of doctrine. In order to make clear the difference between law and grace, a writer argued that if a murderer came to him and inquired how to be saved, he would not say, "Turn away from your old life, cease to commit murder and believe on Jesus Christ." That, said the writer, would be mixing law and grace. All he could say to be scriptural, he reasoned, would be, "Believe on the Lord Jesus Christ and you will be saved." Such unholy teaching could not possibly come directly from the Scriptures—it could only result from the writer's frightened retreat from the error of salvation by works.

We have noticed much the same thing in our standard attitudes toward science, evolution and various current philosophies that we believe to be contrary or unsympathetic to the Christian faith. Our reaction to those enemies is one of blind flight. We use up a lot of ammunition, but we waste it in a rear guard action that can at best only slow up what is too patently a retreat.

It is our firm faith that Christianity can stand on its own legs. Christ does not need our nervous defense. The church must not allow itself to be maneuvered into fighting its enemy's war, letting the unbelieving world decide what it is to believe and where and when it is to act. Just as long as the church does this, it is falling short of its privileges in Christ Jesus.

"Ye shall receive power," (Acts 1:8) said our Lord to His disciples, and "power" means "ability to do." It is God's purpose to give us ample power to carry the fight to the enemy instead of sitting by passively allowing the enemy to carry the fight to us. If anyone is to go on the defensive, it should never be the church. The truth is self-validating and self-renewing—its whole psychology is that of attack. Its own vigorous attack is all the defense it needs.

Could it be that the deep cause behind all this frightened defensive action on the part of evangelicals today is the failure of so many leaders to have a true spiritual experience of their own? It is hard to see how any man or woman who has seen heaven opened and heard the voice of God speaking to his or her own heart can ever be uncertain about the message he or she is to proclaim.

Easter Meditation

There is an exquisite appropriateness in our celebrating the resurrection of Christ in the spring. When nature is waking to life again after her long winter of sleep, it is then that the thoughts of Christians everywhere are turned to the wonder of the Savior's coming out of the tomb after His ordeal with sin and death. Christ's resurrection was an act once accomplished at a given moment in history. It does not in any sense depend upon seasons or celebrations, nor does the miracle of the springtime add anything to the glory of the once-done deed. The workings of God in nature do, however, cast a warm light upon His workings in redemption and the springtime of life in the earth illustrates the miracle of life in the new creation.

Nicolas Herman, at eighteen years of age, was brought to Christ by seeing in midwinter a dry and leafless tree and thinking what a change the spring would make in its condition. He reasoned that if God could make such a difference in a tree, He could change the heart of a sinner, too, and God did not fail him. His heart was changed, and from that day his life was devoted to the service of Christ. Uncounted thousands of Christians over the last 300 years have thanked God that young Nicolas saw that leafless tree.

It takes some faith to stand in a winter landscape surrounded by the chill silence of snow and ice and believe that in a few short weeks every trace of frost will be gone, that the snow-covered hills will be dressed in green and the ice-blocked streams will be running swift and free again in the summer sun. Yet our confidence is never disappointed. "The earth is the LORD's" (Exodus 9:29) and "thou [God] renewest the face of the earth" (Psalm 104:30).

It is hard to imagine anything less hopeful than the sight of a burial. When the body of Christ was taken down from the cross, wrapped in a clean linen cloth and laid in a new tomb hewn out of the rock, how many who looked on had the faith to hope that inside three days this dead Man would be walking again among men and women, alive forevermore? But so it came to pass. Aaron's rod budded. The leafless tree on which the Savior died sprang into bloom. What had been stark death before became life at the touch of God, and the gallows became the gate to everlasting life.

The resurrection of Christ, we repeat, is a once-done act. "Knowing that Christ being raised from the dead dieth no more; death hath no more dominion over him" (Romans 6:9). But Christians die. Every day the bodies of believing men and women are taken out to the cemetery and laid to rest with quiet songs and soft repetitions of Scripture. No matter how we may try to avoid the facts, Christians die as their Lord died before them. Their cold helplessness, their sudden strange silence, which no pleadings of anguished love can break, their apparent defeat by the relentless forces of nature—all this stuns the heart and (if the truth were told) arouses uncomfortable fears that this is all, that we have seen our friends for the last time. It is winter when we lay our loved ones down. So it seems to the natural heart. So it must have appeared to some of the Thessalonian Christians. Why otherwise would it have been necessary for Paul to write and exhort them not to sorrow as others who had no hope?

One thing the resurrection teaches us is that we must not trust appearances. The leafless tree says by its appearance that there will be no second spring. The body in Joseph's new tomb appears to signify the end of everything for Christ and His disciples. The limp form of a newly dead believer suggests everlasting defeat. Yet how wrong are all these appearances. The tree will bloom again. Christ arose the third day according to the Scriptures, and the Christian will rise at the shout of the Lord and the voice of the archangel.

Faith can afford to accept the appearance of defeat, knowing the true believer cannot be defeated finally. "Because I live, ye shall live also" (John 14:19). That is the message of Easter. What a blessed message for the whole world if men would only believe it.

The Importance of Direction

In the Christian way, the one vital thing is not speed nor distance attained, but direction. For this reason the Scriptures exhort the runner to patience and say nothing about speed. The Lord would seem to be more concerned with *where* we are going rather than *how fast*. A steady pace in the right direction will lead to the right goal at last, but if the life is aimed at the wrong goal, speed will only take us further astray in a shorter time.

Lack of direction is the cause of many tragic failures in religious activities. The churches are overrun with persons of both sexes (though the vast majority are men) who have never known a clear call of God to anything in particular. Such people are often victims of whim and chance, the easy prey of ambitious leaders who seek to gain prominence by using others for their own ends. The directionless Christian is the one who supports the new and spectacular, regardless of whether or not it is in accord with the Scriptures and the revealed will of God.

A great economizing of time and effort can be effected by learning what we should do and then sticking to it, quietly refusing to be turned aside from our task. Paul said, "But one thing I do," and by paring his activities down to an important minimum he multiplied his efficiency many times over. We must avoid the error of assuming that because we are busy we are therefore getting a lot done. Much of our current activity is in line with the old gentleman who got his peg leg caught in a hole in the sidewalk and walked around it all night trying to get home.

The further we get from our beginnings, the stronger the temptation to surrender to the confused ways of modern fundamentalism and play ring-around-a-rosy with whatever partners happen to be popular at the moment. This temptation we must resist with everything in us. Should we take up the ways of the blind twentieth century church, we will surely waste our time and other people's money in the mistaken belief that we are doing the will of God. From such a major calamity, O Lord, deliver us.

If we should seem at times to be a bit slow, let it be remembered that we do know the direction we are called to go, and as long as we have followed that original urge we have been blessed with success beyond our best expectation. That we maintain our God-revealed direction is vitally important. Let us not fail here.

Faber's "Good Confession"

Several years ago I discovered a Christian testimony, which for sheer beauty is hardly matched by anything in religious literature. This lyric confession was given by Frederic W. Faber, author of "Faith of Our Fathers," "There's a Wideness in God's Mercy," "Jesus! Jesus! Dearest Lord" and many other loved hymns. It appears to be just about the most perfect combination of restrained dignity and joyous abandonment that can be found in evangelical literature. It would be equally at home in the quiet study of the mystic or in the rough tabernacle of the camp meeting.

In reading this confession we should guard against the feeling that Faber's experience was unique. Because we never heard it put like this before, we may be tempted to assume that there have not been many people so radically and soundly converted as was Faber. This would be an error in judgment. Millions have been as wonderfully converted as Faber, but only one in a million has the gift of self-expression to tell out his or her experience so completely and with such exquisite perfection.

A recent writer has remarked that next to the power to create great art is the power to enjoy it. The mind that can best appreciate Bach or da Vinci or Milton is nearest in capacity to the genius himself. So the Christian who can understand and enjoy a testimony such as this may not be too far removed from the spiritual attitude of the man who wrote it. The earthly soul will not feel at home with Faber.

It is our cheerful belief that thousands of men and women who will read these words have met God in a revolutionary, transforming encounter fully equal to that of Faber's. What they have lacked is the gift of self-analysis and the literary craftsmanship that would enable them to write of it in such ecstatic language.

Here it is. Faber called it "A Good Confession."

> The chains that have bound me are flung
>   to the wind,
>
>   By the mercy of God the poor slave is set
>   free;
>   And the strong grace of heaven breathes
>   fresh o'er the mind,
>   Like the bright winds of summer that
>   gladden the sea.

There was nought in God's world half so
  dark or so vile
 As the sin and bondage that fettered my
  soul;
There was nought half so base as the
  malice and guile
 Of my own sordid passions, or Satan's
  control.

For years I have borne about hell in my
  breast;

 When I thought of my God it was
  nothing but gloom;
Day brought me no pleasure, night gave
  me no rest,
 There was still the grim shadow of
  horrible doom.

It seemed as if nothing less likely could be
 Than that light should break in on a
  dungeon so deep;
To create a new world were less hard than
  to free
 The slave from his bondage, the soul
  from its sleep.

But the Word had gone forth, and said, Let
  there be light,
 And it flashed through my soul like a
  sharp passing smart;
One look to my Savior, and all the dark

night,
Like a dream scarce remembered, was
gone from my heart.

I cried out for mercy, and fell on my knees,

And confessed, while my heart with

keen sorrow was wrung;
'Twas the labor of minutes, and years of
disease
Fell as fast from my soul as the words from
my tongue.

And now, blest be God and the sweet Lord
who died!
No deer on the mountain, no bird in the
sky,
No bright wave that leaps on the dark
bounding tide,
Is a creature so free or so happy as I.

All hail, then, all hail, to the dear Precious
Blood,
That hath worked these sweet wonders of
mercy in me;
May each day countless numbers throng
down to its flood,
And God have His glory, and sinners go
free.

Let's Watch Our Conversation

Most Christians, I find, help each other very little in ordinary conversation, and often do each other much harm. There are few who can talk for any length of time without descending to speech that is not only unprofitable but positively harmful.

That is a flaw in our lives that should be dealt with seriously. It often happens that all the good effect of a service will be destroyed by light and unworthy conversation after the meeting. This is a sad fault, for the ministry of any church should be no more than a public expression of the pure spirituality that is the regular day-by-day life of those who are a part of it.

The minister himself should simply carry into the pulpit on Sunday the same spirit that has characterized him all week long. He should not need to adopt another voice nor speak in a different tone. The subject matter would necessarily differ from that of his ordinary conversation, but the mood and attitude expressed in his sermons should be identical to his daily living.

Harmful or vain speech blocks revival and grieves the Spirit more than we are likely to realize. It destroys the accumulative effect of spiritual impressions and makes it necessary each Sunday to recapture the devotional mood that has been lost during the week. Thus we are compelled constantly to do over again the work of last week and to retake ground lost by unprofitable conversation.

It is not desirable that we form the habit of constant religious chatter when we meet with our friends. There is no surer proof of our basic levity of character than the careless way religion is often discussed among us. I do not plead for more religious talk—religious shoptalk can be as dull and boring as any other shoptalk, and what is worse, it may become insincere and meaningless. The ideal to aim at is a chaste, natural and love-washed conversation at all times, whether we are discussing things on earth or things in heaven.

We Must Have Spiritual Leadership Again

Someone wrote to the godly Macarius of Optino that his spiritual counsel had been helpful. "This cannot be," Macarius wrote in reply. "Only the mistakes are mine. All good advice is the advice of the Spirit of God, His advice that I happened to have heard rightly and to have passed on without distorting it."

There is an excellent lesson here that we must not allow to go unregarded. It is the sweet humility of the man of God. "Only the mistakes are mine." He was fully convinced that his own efforts could result only in mistakes, and that any good that came of his advice must be the work of the Holy Spirit operating within him. Apparently this was more than a sudden impulse of self-depreciation, which the proudest of men may at times feel—it was rather a settled conviction with him, a conviction that gave direction to his entire life. His long and humble ministry, which brought spiritual aid to multitudes, reveals this clearly enough.

In this day when shimmering "personalities" carry on the Lord's work after the methods of the entertainment world, it is refreshing to associate for even a moment in the pages of a book with a sincere and humble man who keeps his own personality out of sight and places the emphasis on the inworking of God. It is our belief that the evangelical movement will continue to drift further and further from the New Testament position until its leadership passes from the modern religious star to the self-effacing saint, who asks for no praise and seeks no place, happy only when the glory is attributed to God, and he is forgotten.

Until such men as these return again to spiritual leadership, we may expect a progressive deterioration in the quality of popular Christianity until we reach the point where the grieved Holy Spirit withdraws like the Shechinah from the temple, and we are left like Jerusalem after the crucifixion—God-deserted and alone. In spite of every effort to torture doctrine to prove that the Spirit will not forsake religious men, the record reveals plainly enough that He sometimes does. He has in the past forsaken groups when they had gone too far to make a recovery.

It is an open question whether or not the evangelical movement has sinned too long and departed too far from God to return again to spiritual sanity.

Personally I do not believe it is too late to repent, if the so-called Christians of the day would repudiate evil leadership and seek God again in true penitence and tears. The *if* is the big problem—will they? Or are they too well satisfied with religious frolic and froth even to recognize their sad departure from the New Testament faith? If the latter is true, then there is nothing left but judgment.

The devil is adept at the use of the red herring. He knows well how to divert the attention of the praying Christian from his subtler but deadly attacks to something more obvious and less harmful. Then while the soldiers of the Lord gather excitedly at one gate, he quietly enters by another. And when the "saints" lose interest in the red herring, they return to find the newly baptized and pious enemy in charge of proceedings. So far are they from recognizing him that they soon adopt his ways and call it progress.

Within the last quarter of a century, we have actually seen a major shift in the beliefs and practices of the evangelical wing of the church so radical as to amount to a complete sell-out—and all this behind the cloak of fervent orthodoxy. With a Bible under their arm and a bundle of tracts in their pocket, religious people now meet to carry on "services" so carnal, so pagan, that they can hardly be distinguished from the old vaudeville shows of earlier days. And for a preacher or an editor to challenge this heresy is to invite ridicule and abuse from every quarter.

Our only hope is that renewed spiritual pressure will be exerted increasingly by self-effacing and courageous men and women who desire nothing but the glory of God and the purity of the church. May God send us many of them. They are long overdue.

The Christian
Is the True Realist

Some shallow thinkers dismiss the Christian as an unrealistic person who lives in a make-believe world. "Religion," they say, "is a flight from reality. To embrace it is to take refuge in dreams."

By constantly arguing this way, they have managed to disturb a great many people and to create in many minds a gnawing doubt concerning the soundness of the Christian position. But there is nothing to be disturbed about—a better acquaintance with the facts will dispel all doubts and convince believers that their expectations are valid and their faith is well grounded.

If realism is the recognition of things as they really are, Christians are of all people the most realistic. They of all intelligent thinkers are the most concerned with reality. They insist that their beliefs correspond with facts. They pare things down to their stark essentials and squeeze out of their minds everything that inflates their thinking. They demand to know the whole truth about God, sin, life, death, moral accountability and the world to come. They want to know the worst about themselves in order that they may do something about it. Something in them refuses to be cheated, however pleasant the self-deception might be to their self-esteem. They take into account the undeniable fact that they have sinned. They recognize the shortness of time and the certainty of death. These they do not try to avoid nor alter to their own liking. These are facts and they face them full on. They are realists!

We of the Christian faith need not go on the defensive. The burden of proof lies with the opponent. The charge of unrealism is one which can be brought against the unbeliever with unanswerable logic.

The man or woman of the world is the dreamer, not the Christian. Sinners can never be quite themselves. They must pretend all their lives. They must act as if they were never going to die, and yet they know too well that they will. They must act as if they have never sinned, when deep in their hearts, they know very well that they have. They must act unconcerned about God and judgment and the future life, and all the time their hearts are deeply disturbed about their precarious condition. They must keep up a front of nonchalance while shrinking from facts and wincing under the lash of conscience. The news of a friend's sudden death leaves them shaken with the suggestion that they may be next, but they dare not show this—they must cover their terror as best they can and continue to act their part. All their adult lives, they must dodge and hide and conceal. When they finally drop the act, they either lose their mind, turn to Christ or try suicide.

Say, poor worldling, can it be
That my heart should envy thee?

Praying Till We Pray

Dr. Moody Stuart, a great praying man of a past generation, once drew up a set of rules to guide him in his prayers. Among these rules is this one: "Pray till you pray."

The difference between praying till you quit and praying till you pray is illustrated by the American evangelist John Wesley Lee. He often likened a season of prayer to a church service, and insisted that many of us close the meeting before the service is over. He confessed that once he arose too soon from a prayer session and started down the street to take care of some pressing business. He had only gone a short distance when an inner voice reproached him. "Son," the voice seemed to say, "did you not pronounce the benediction before the meeting was ended?" He understood, and at once hurried back to the place of prayer where he tarried till the burden lifted and the blessing came down.

The habit of breaking off our prayers before we have truly prayed is as common as it is unfortunate. Often the last ten minutes may mean more to us than the first half hour, because we must spend a long time getting into the proper mood to pray effectively. We may need to struggle with our thoughts to draw them in from where they have been scattered through the multitude of distractions that result from the task of living in a disordered world.

Here, as elsewhere in spiritual matters, we must be sure to distinguish the ideal from the real. Ideally we should be living moment-by-moment in a state of such perfect union with God that no special preparation is necessary. But actually there are few who can honestly say that this is their experience. Candor will compel most of us to admit that we often experience a struggle before we can escape from the emotional alienation and sense of unreality that sometimes settle over us as a sort of prevailing mood.

Whatever a dreamy idealism may say, we are forced to deal with things down on the level of practical reality. If when we come to prayer our hearts feel dull and unspiritual, we should not try to argue ourselves out of it. Rather, we should admit it frankly and pray our way through. Some Christians smile at the thought of "praying through," but something of the same idea is found in the writings of practically every great praying saint from Daniel to the present day. We cannot afford to stop praying till we have actually prayed.

Obedience: A Neglected Doctrine

There is what William James called "a certain blindness in human beings" that prevents us from seeing what we do not want to see. This, along with the direct work of the devil himself, may account for the fact that the doctrine of obedience is so largely neglected in modern religious circles. That God expects us to be "obedient children" (1 Peter 1:14) is admitted, of course, but it is seldom stressed sufficiently to get action. Many people seem to feel that our obligation to obey has been discharged by the act of believing on Jesus Christ at the beginning of our Christian lives.

We should remember that "the will is the seat of true religion in the soul." Nothing genuine has been done in a man or woman's life until his or her will has been surrendered in active obedience. It was disobedience that brought about the ruin of the race. It is the "obedience of faith" that brings us back again into divine favor.

A world of confusion and disappointment results from trying to believe without obeying. This puts us in the position of a bird trying to fly with one wing folded. We merely flap in a circle and seek to cheer our hearts with the hope that the whirling ball of feathers is proof that a revival is under way. A good deal of praying at our camp meeting altars has the identical effect of a good cry. It releases pent-up emotions and relaxes tense nerves. The smile that follows is accepted by the eager helpers as evidence that a deep spiritual work has been done. This can be for some people a tragic error, resulting in permanent injury and loss to the spiritual life.

A mere passive surrender may be no surrender at all. Any real submission to the will of God must include willingness to take orders from Him from that time on. When the heart is irrevocably committed to receiving and obeying orders from the Lord Himself, a specific work has been done, but not until then. We are not likely to see among us any remarkable transformations of individuals or churches until the Lord's ministers again give to obedience the place of prominence it occupies in the Scriptures.

Honorary Christians

Sometimes we hear of a politician or other ce-
lebrity who is made a "chief" of one or another tribe of American Indians. He is greeted
solemnly, powwowed over in guttural tones, in-
vested with a gaudy headdress of eagle feathers,
has his picture taken with the big men of the tribe
and is from that time on a chief among them.

His self-conscious smirk tells us plainly that he
considers the whole thing a joke, but the unsmiling
Indians apparently take it all pretty seriously. It requires no great penetration to see that all the ceremonies, beads, feathers and powwows in the world
cannot make an Indian out of a white man. At the
most he is only an honorary chief, not a real one.

Compare this to many evangelical churches,
which have altogether too many members who
are Christians by initiation, not by spiritual birth.
They have been powwowed over by the local sa-

chems and given the impression that they are Christians in fact, when the truth is that they are Christians only in name.

All the religious ceremonies invented by the prolific minds of all the religious leaders of the world cannot make a Christian out of a sinner. No man, regardless of how rich and mysterious his robes may be, can make a Christian out of another man. The impressive appointments of the beautiful church and the solemn rites of the sanctuary are merely the Grand Sachem's tepee on a vaster scale. The best that we can hope for there is religion by initiation. Seekers come out only as honorary Christians. The root of life is not in them—and they deserve more pity.

Our Lord tells us plainly that we must be born again before we can enter the kingdom of God. Let us not be satisfied with honorary membership in the kingdom. And let us not take anything for granted. There is too much at stake in this vital area of our lives.

CHAPTER

29

Let's Give Generously, but Wisely

The amount of money wasted in religious work each year can never by accurately computed, but it must run into the millions of dollars in the United States alone. One of the liabilities of our free Protestant system is the absence of effective checks to prevent irresponsible people from launching into any religious venture they see fit and appealing to the Christian public to pay their bills. The result of this kind of freedom is that racketeering has long since invaded the field of religion and countless numbers of self-anointed prophets are living high at the expense of the saints.

I do not have in mind the huge amounts of money spent to propagate the many false cults that are flourishing like lush weeds in our rich American soil. I confine my considerations to that area of religious activity that passes for New Testament Christianity. The facts indicate that all is not well even there.

A number of factors have combined in recent years to encourage irregularities in the field of religious work to make it possible for disreputable persons to grow fat at the expense of the generous Christian public. First and foremost is the extraordinary financial prosperity that the nation now enjoys. Almost everyone these days has plenty of money to donate to religious and charitable purposes, and it is not human nature to permit such a rich bonanza to lie untouched, when it is so easy to latch onto large chunks of it by launching some religious enterprise and calling upon good people to support it.

Another factor is the amazing speed of transportation and communication that modern science has made available to all. The printing press, our rapid mail service, the radio, the movie and the now-popular religious drama have made it possible to reach the Christian with mass appeals for money with complete assurance that those appeals will bring in handsome amounts of the coveted green stuff. Many of these appeals are accompanied by bold claims of unusual faith. One gets the impression that these valiant warriors are ready to step into any arena to do battle with the enemies of the Lord with nothing to protect them but the shining shield of faith. The blunt fact is that most of the adventures are based upon nothing more spiritual than a shrewd knowledge of the proven generosity of God's people.

It is to the everlasting credit of God's children that they can be moved to sacrificial giving by a touching story or the sight of human suffering. It is only necessary to fly around the world and return with pictures of human misery, and God's dear sheep will promptly go down on their hunkers and permit themselves to be sheared down to the skin by persons morally unworthy to clean out the sheep pen. The tenderhearted saints think with their feelings and pour out consecrated wealth indiscriminately on projects wholly unworthy of their support. Most Christians are hesitant to question the honesty of anyone who says complimentary things about the Lord and perspires when he preaches. To such they give vast amounts of money and never ask for nor expect an accounting. This speaks well for their hearts but does not say too much in favor of their spiritual discernment.

Knowing how sensitive we Americans are about our right to decide when and where we shall give and whom we shall support, I do not expect my readers to take this admonition lying down. I am prepared to be told that I am interfering in matters that do not concern me. My answer is that I personally know that there are scores of godly pastors who privately deplore the exploitation of God's people by disreputable persons but who are too timid to say so publicly. Fools rush in where angels fear to tread, and if these angels will not speak up to protect the saints then someone less fearful (if less angelic) must do so.

Furthermore, we must all make an accounting to God for our disposal of the wealth we enjoy. Giving to further dishonest projects is wasting God's money, and in the great day we will tell God why we did it. It will pay us to use prayerful caution before we make our gifts. Let us not give less, but let us give more wisely. Some day we'll be glad we did.

Symptomatic Words: "Fair," "Unfair"

Words mean only what the user intends them to mean, and I do not want to make any word "guilty by association." Yet every mood has its characteristic verbal expression and when a given word is used we may with some accuracy assume that a certain mood is present also. For this reason words may be said to be symptomatic. They are not themselves health or disease, but they may well indicate the presence of either. They may also indicate what kind of disease the user is suffering from or the degree of health he or she enjoys.

This observation is the result of listening to religious people talk. After hearing some Christians talk for a while, one begins to sense the presence of health or disease in their souls. Certain words keep cropping up that tell us more about the speakers than they dream we know, and certainly more than they want us to know. Words are symptomatic.

One such word sometimes used among Christians is "fair," or its unpleasant sister "unfair." People use these words to describe the treatment accorded them by other people, and on the surface they would seem to be altogether innocent, even indispensible words. Nevertheless, they indicate an inner attitude that has no place among Christians. The man who refers to one or another act as being "unfair" to him is not a victorious man. He is inwardly defeated, and in self-defense he is appealing to the referee to note that he has been fouled. This gives him an alibi when they carry him out on a stretcher and saves his face while his bruises heal. He can always blame his defeat on the fact that he was treated unfairly by others.

Christians who understand the true meaning of the cross will never whine about being treated unfairly. Whether or not they are given fair treatment will never enter their heads. They know they have been called to follow Christ, and certainly Christ did not receive anything remotely approaching fair treatment from mankind. Right there lies the glory of the cross—that a Man suffered unfairly, was abused and maligned and crucified by people unworthy to breathe the same air with Him. Yet He did not open His mouth. Though reviled He did not return the hatred, and when He suffered, He did not threaten anyone. The thought of His shouting for fair play simply cannot be entertained by the reverent heart. His whole life was dedicated to restoring that which He had not taken away. Had He sat down and calculated how much He owed and then carefully paid no more, the whole moral universe would have collapsed.

The victorious Christian is not concerned with getting his or her fair share of things. Love is not self-seeking, and the odd thing is that the happy saint who opens his or her hand to be robbed at the will of others will always be found to be richer than those who do the robbing.

Sometimes, it is true, God allows His people to suffer unjudged wrongs and waits for the day of reckoning to balance the scales. But usually His judgments are not so long postponed. And even granted that Christians must suffer wrongs here below, if they take them in a good spirit and without complaint, they have conquered their enemy and won the fight. It is their first desire to be inwardly victorious, and if they are able to laugh and love and praise when they are being mistreated, they have attained their hearts' desire. Who could ask for more?

More Symptomatic Words: "Resent," "Resentment"

I n the previous chapter it was stated that there are telltale words that carry meanings not included in their etymology. The word "unfair" was cited as being such a word. "Resent" in its various forms is another.

I have been around religious circles quite awhile now, and I have never heard the word "resent" used by victorious Christians. Or at least if they used the word, it was not to express any feelings within their own heart. In the course of scores of conferences and hundreds of conversations, I have many times heard people say, "I resent that," but I repeat—I have never heard the words used by victorious Christians. Resentment simply cannot dwell in a loving heart. Before resentfulness can enter, love must take its flight and bitterness must enter.

The bitter soul will compile a list of slights at which it takes offense and will watch over itself like a mother bear over her cubs. And the figure is apt, for the resentful heart is always surly and suspicious like a she-bear.

Few sights are more depressing than that of a professed Christian defending his or her supposed rights and bitterly resisting any attempt to violate them. Such a Christian has never accepted the way of the cross. The sweet graces of meekness and humility are unknown to that person. Every day he or she grows harder and more acrimonious, trying to defend his or her reputation, rights, ministry against his or her imagined foes.

The only cure for this sort of thing is to die to self and rise with Christ into newness of life. The man or woman who sets the will of God as his or her goal will reach that goal not by self-defense but by self-abnegation. Then no matter what sort of treatment that person receives from other people, he or she will be altogether at peace. The will of God has been done—this Christian does not care whether it comes with curses or compliments, for he or she does not seek one or the other, but wants to do the will of God at any cost. Then, whether riding the crest of public favor or wallowing in the depth of obscurity, he or she will be content. If there be some who take pleasure in holding this Christian down, still he or she will not resent them, for he or she seeks not advancement but the will of God.

It is sad that certain pagan philosophers have had to teach us Christians so simple a lesson as this. "I must die," said Epictetus, "and must I die groaning too? I must be exiled; and what hinders me, then, but that I may go smiling, and cheerful, and serene? 'Betray a secret.' I will not betray it. 'Then I will fetter you.' You will fetter my leg, but no one can get the better of my free will. 'I will behead that paltry body of yours.' Did I ever tell you," answered Epictetus, "that I alone had a head that couldn't be cut off?

"This is to have studied what ought to be studied; to have placed our desires and aversions above tyranny and above chance. I must die—if instantly, I will die instantly; if in a short time, I will dine first, and when the hour comes, then I will die. How? As becomes one who restores what is not his own."

Let no one reject the reasoning of this sturdy old philosopher. Even without the light of saving grace, he knew how a created being ought to behave beneath the mighty hand of its Creator, and that is more than many Christians appear to know. But we have better authority than his for our conduct. Christ left us an example, and from it there can be no appeal. As He was, so are we in this world, and He never felt a trace of resentment against any man. Even those who crucified Him were forgiven while they were in the act. Not a word did He utter against them or against the liars and hypocrites who stirred them up to destroy Him. Just how evil they all were He knew better than any other man, but He maintained toward them an attitude of charitable understanding. They were only doing their duty and even those who ordered them to their grisly task were unaware of the meaning of it all. To Pilate He said, "Thou couldest have no power at all against me, except it were given thee from above" (John 19:11). So He referred everything back to the will of God and rose above the swamp-land of personalities. He held no grudge against any man. He felt no resentment.

The worst feature about this whole thing is that it does no good to call attention to it. The bitter heart is not likely to recognize its own condition, and if the resentful man reads this editorial at all, he will smile smugly and think I mean someone else. In the meantime he will grow smaller and smaller trying to get big, and will become more and more obscure trying to become known. As he pushes on toward his selfish goal, his prayers will be accusations against the Almighty and his whole relationship toward other Christians will be one of suspicion and distrust.

As Spurgeon said of someone, "May the grass grow green on his grave when he dies, for nothing ever grew around him while he lived."

CHAPTER

32

The Prophet Is a Man Apart

The church is God's witness to each generation, and its ministers are its voice. Through them it becomes vocal. By them it has always spoken to the world, and by them God has spoken to the church itself. The testimony of the church's godly laymen has ever been a mighty aid in the work it seeks to accomplish, but its laymen can never do, and assuredly are not called to do, the work of its ministers. By gift and calling, the minister is a man apart.

It is not enough, however, that the man of God preach the truth. He has no right to take up a man or woman's time telling him or her what is merely true. It is a doubtful compliment to any preacher to nod the head and say, "That is true." The same might properly be said if he were reciting the multiplication table—that is also true. A church can wither as surely under the ministry of soulless Bible exposition as it can where no Bible is given at all. To

93

be effective, the preacher's message must be alive—it must alarm, arouse challenge; it must be God's present voice to a particular people. Then, and not until then, is it the prophetic word and the man himself, a prophet.

To perfectly fulfill his calling, the prophet must be under the constant sway of the Holy Spirit. Further, he must be alert to moral and spiritual conditions. All spiritual teaching should relate to life. It should intrude into the daily and private living of the hearers. Without being personal, the true prophet will nevertheless pierce the conscience of each listener as if the message had been directed to him alone.

To preach the truth it is often necessary that the man of God know the people's hearts better than they themselves do. People are frequently confused inwardly—the anointed prophet must speak to this confusion with clarifying wisdom. He must surprise his hearers with his unsuspected knowledge of their secret thoughts.

The work of a minister is altogether too difficult for any man. We are driven to God for wisdom. We must seek the mind of Christ and throw ourselves on the Holy Spirit for spiritual and mental acumen equal to the task.

It's Not a One-Way Street

Agreat deal is heard these days about the number of young men, particularly seminary students, who give up their faith in the Scriptures and go over theologically to the so-called liberal position. That hundreds of young men begin as lukewarm evangelicals and after a year or so under the tutelage of unbelieving professors turn their backs upon the faith of their fathers cannot be denied. And we have no wish to deny it here. It is always better to look facts in the face, however unpleasant the sight may be. The traffic between faith and unbelief is tragically heavy, as the Scripture declared it would be. But we may encourage our hearts with the knowledge that the traffic does not always move in the direction of unbelief—sometimes it moves the other way.

Every now and then the cheering news comes to us of some "liberal" who gets sick to his stomach with the plum pudding philosophy and the mixture of cheap poetry and applied psychology they have been fed by the modernists and comes home like the prodigal to the Father's house. I have heard of a number of such persons over the last few years, and undoubtedly there are hundreds of others of whom I have not heard. Proof that the traffic is not all one way is afforded by the following testimony. This is part of a letter written to a friend by the recently converted pastor of a denominational church. It speaks for itself.

"Up until last summer I was just one of the proud, unsaved, 'liberal' false prophets, preaching a gospel that is no gospel, but only the cheap sentimentalism that the world calls religion.

"Three months ago the Lord saved me and has made me, even me, a new creation in Christ Jesus. Last summer I began to sicken of the unitarian pantheism that I was preaching in the name of Christ. I rebelled against it and began preaching—still blindly—about sin and salvation by faith, all the while confused and upset. I found a new friend who began to help me in an intellectual way to throw off the trappings of liberalism.

"Then, one day God took a veil off my understanding, and I suddenly knew that Jesus Christ died my death—that He has died the death I am due to die because of my sin—but that if I accepted Him as Lord and Savior I would not have to die! I surrendered myself and gave up all, that I might be His bond slave. And Jesus Christ accepted me and came into my empty self and took my life for Himself. How gracious and wonderful He is!

"I just wanted you to know that this has happened to me by the grace of God in Christ. Every man must be born of the Spirit, and when by faith God gives him this unspeakable gift, he knows it, for the Spirit Himself bears witness to our spirit, and we know in whom we have believed.

"My people here need to be saved. Some of them truly know the Lord Jesus Christ, but so many need to hear the message of another witness. I pray that the Holy Spirit will come with fire and power to baptize those who will believe."

An encouraging thought for the true Christian is that the movement from orthodoxy to liberalism is usually slow, almost too slow to be perceived, whereas the movement back to faith is sudden. Unbelief enters the soul by a slow seepage; the toxin gets through the walls of the soul by a kind of spiritual osmosis so that the victim is well poisoned before he or she notices it, and the pathological condition that results usually makes it impossible for that person to know what is wrong. *I have never known of a single instance where a man or woman accepted modernism as a result of a spiritual experience.* Rather it is the lack of such experience that exposes the soul to the in-seeping of the poison of unbelief.

The movement from doubt to faith, conversely, is usually sudden, often explosive. A man or woman is *converted* to Christ by a sudden, violent encounter with God and spiritual things. This person's conversation becomes an enlightening, a sudden inward illumination that shows the certainties of the spiritual life as sharply as a midnight landscape when illumined by a flash of lightning. After long and painful searching of the heart, after what may be an agony of wrestling with the angel, the morning breaks suddenly as it broke on Jacob. There is no doubt about it now. The heart can say, "What have I to do any more with idols? I have heard him, and observed him" (Hosea 14:8).

The simple fact that the believer *always experiences* something and the unbeliever *never does* should tell us a great deal. The liberal can never be quite sure of anything—it is contrary to his or her whole philosophy to be certain. Only the true Christian is sure. He or she has seen the sun rise, and it takes more than the contentions of the pseudo-learned to destroy the brightness of this person's faith.

The Holy Spirit Is Here

Pentecost did not come and go—Pentecost came and stayed. Chronologically the day may be found on the historic calendar; dynamically it remains with us in all its fullness of power.

Today is the day of Pentecost. With the blessed Holy Spirit there is no Yesterday or Tomorrow—there is only the everlasting Now. And since He is altogether God, enjoying all the attributes of the Godhead, there is with Him no Elsewhere; He inhabits an eternal Here. His center is Everywhere; His bound is Nowhere. It is impossible to leave His presence, though it is possible to have Him withdraw the manifestation of that presence.

Our insensibility to the presence of the Spirit is one of the greatest losses that our unbelief and preoccupation have cost us. We have made Him a tenet of our creed, we have enclosed Him in a religious word, but we have known Him little in personal experience. Satan has hindered us all he could by raising conflicting opinions about the Spirit, by making Him a topic for hot and uncharitable debate between Christians. In the meanwhile our hearts crave Him, and we hardly know what the craving means.

It would help us if we could remember that the Spirit is Himself God, the very nature of the Godhead subsisting in a form that can impart itself to our consciousness. We know only as much of the other Persons of the Trinity as He reveals to us. It is His light upon the face of Christ, which enables us to know Him. It is His light within us, which enables us to understand the Scriptures. Without Him the Word of truth is only darkness.

The Spirit is sent to be our Friend, to guide us over the long way home. He is Christ's own Self come to live with us, allowing Him to fulfill His word, "Lo, I am with you alway," (Matthew 28:20) even while He sits at the right hand of the Majesty in the heavens.

It will be a new day for us when we put away false notions and foolish fears and allow the Holy Spirit to fellowship with us as intimately as He wants to do, to talk to us as Christ talked to His disciples by the Sea of Galilee. After that there can be no more loneliness, only the glory of the never-failing Presence.

CHAPTER

35

The Angel of the Commonplace

The story of Zechariah and the angel (Luke 1:11-22) suggests that people in these strange days are seeing things badly out of focus. It takes real effort of the mind to wrestle loose from the false philosophies that hold the masses of mankind in their grasp.

Thinking only of America for the moment, it may be said with complete accuracy that the masses of our population think the same about almost everything. Our boasted right to disagree is a joke to the one who can see past the end of his own nose. Except for the numerically unimportant rebels among us, we Americans react alike toward our social stimuli. We are as carefully conditioned as were the people of Germany under Hitler or the Russians under Stalin. The difference is that our conditioning is accomplished not by force but by advertising and other media of mass education. The press, the radio and the various dramatic forms, among which the movie is the most potent, have brainwashed the average American as successfully as was ever done by the totalitarian propaganda machines. Of course there were no threats, no concentration camps and no secret police, but the job is done nevertheless. And the proof of its effectiveness is found in the fact that those so washed are not aware of what has happened to them, and will greet any such notion with loud guffaws. But whether the victim laughs or weeps, he or she is still a victim.

One ominous sign of our warped concepts is our false attitude toward the ordinary. There has grown up around us an idea that the commonplace is old-fashioned and strictly for the birds. Hardly anything is permitted to be just what it is—everything these days must be "processed." On some levels of society, for instance, the sight of a mother nursing her baby would evoke exclamations of wonder if not downright disapproval. Have not the manufacturers invented better baby food than mother's milk? And anyway, such food has not been "processed," nor is it produced in a union shop. And how can Mrs. America be glamorous when engaged in such a lowly and commonplace occupation?

The mania after glamor and the contempt of the ordinary are signs and portents in American society. Even religion has gone glamorous. And in case you do not know what glamor is, I might explain that it is a compound of sex, paint, padding and artificial lights. It came to America by way of the honky-tonk and the movie lot, got accepted by the world first and then strutted into the church—vain, self-admiring and contemptuous. Instead of the Spirit of God in our midst, we now have the spirit of glamor, as artificial as painted death and as hollow as the skull, which is its symbol.

That we now have to deal with a new spirit in religion is not merely a figure of speech. The new Christianity has clearly introduced new concepts that face us brazenly wherever we turn within the confines of evangelical Christianity. The plain virtues, so dear to the heart of the prophet and apostle and the substance of the solemn and fiery sermons of our Protestant forebears, have been sent into retirement with the fireman's horse and the blacksmith's bellows. The new Christian no longer wants to be good or saintly or virtuous. He or she wants to be happy and free, to have "peace of mind" and, above all, wants to enjoy the thrills of religion without any of its perils. He or she brings to the New Testament a paganized concept of the Christian way and makes the Scriptures say what he or she wants them to say. And this the new Christian does, oddly enough, while at the same time protesting that he or she is in true lineal descent from the apostles and a true son or daughter of the Reformation. This person's spiritual models are not holy men but ball players, plug-uglies from the prize ring and sentimental but unregenerate stars of anything but heavenly firmament.

True Christianity is built on the Bible, and the Bible is the enemy of all pretense. Simplicity, sincerity and humility are still golden virtues in the kingdom of God. The angel appeared to Zechariah when he was going about his regular prosaic business. There was nothing glamorous about the old saint's task. There was no fanfare, no drama—just a good old man doing what he had been taught. He sought no publicity. The busy people outside paid no attention to him. In this dizzy era is it too much to hope that a few Christians will still believe in the angel of the commonplace?

Let's turn off the colored lights for a while and see what happens. Maybe our eyes will get used to the light of God. And who knows? Maybe someone will again see an angel.

CHAPTER

36

A Rule for Obscure Texts

That there are a few difficult passages in the Bible is well known to everyone. The enemies of the truth are adept at dragging out those obscure verses and holding them as proof that the Bible is a book of mistakes and contradictions. Teachers of false doctrine use them to teach ideas that have no scriptural support. It is well for the true Christian to know what to do with difficult passages.

When reading the Scriptures for our spiritual profit, we would be well advised to pass over the difficult verse without more ado. For instance, the book of First Peter contains 103 verses of blessed, encouraging truth designed to strengthen and instruct the reader. It also contains two verse that are, as Peter said of some of Paul's writing, "hard to understand." Those seeking after God will major on the 103 verses that they can understand and wait for clearer light on the short passages that they find difficult. To do anything else is to create a strong suspicion that we are playing with the Word of God and are glad to discover something to take the heat off our consciences.

The passages in First Peter to which we refer are these: "By which also he went and preached unto the spirits in prison" (3:19), and "For for this cause was the gospel preached also to them that are dead, that they might be judged according to men in the flesh, but live according to God in the spirit" (4:6). That these words are difficult to interpret will not be denied by any humble-minded Bible expositor. Personally I believe I have a satisfactory explanation, but granted that I do not and that I am forced to admit I do not know what they mean, what then?

To answer that, I would give my readers a rule of interpretation that is worthy of universal application when studying the Word of God. It is this: *If I do not know what a difficult passage means, I can at least know what it does not mean.*

It is right here that the false teacher seizes the advantage over the Christian. Let the Christian admit he or she does not know the meaning of a verse and the false teacher eagerly grasps at this admission and pushes it for all it is worth. "You do not know what the verse means? Well, here is what Mrs. Eddy, or Judge Rutherford, or Mrs. Blavatsky, or Joseph Smith says it means. Now you have the meaning. The light has come to you at last." The assurance with which he speaks intimidates the meek soul who has just admitted ignorance of the meaning of the text, and he forthwith surrenders to the guidance of the blind leader.

Let us take a homemade illustration. I am trying to identify a piece of fruit I have just pulled from a tree. It is purple in color, egg-shaped, contains one large pit at its center, has a series of sharp spikes growing all over its surface, has the fragrance of a rose and the taste of watermelon. I shake my head and admit I do not know what it is. Immediately an eager-faced helper appears and says, "If you do not know what it is, I can help you. It is a banana. Now that I have given you the light, come and follow me. I know a lot more things just as wonderful as this."

But I am not so easily fooled. My answer is, "No, my friend, I will not follow you. True, I do not know what this fruit is, *but I surely know what it is not. It is not a banana.*" That will dispose of my little helper most effectively, especially if I can produce a real banana for comparison.

Now what does all this add up to? Simply this—the fact that I may not be able to explain a passage does not obligate me to accept from another an explanation that is obviously phony. *I do not know what it means, but I do know what it does not mean.* I may not know, for instance, what those strange verses mean that tell us about Christ's going in His spirit to preach to the spirits in prison. But I know what they do not mean. They do not mean universal salvation, nor a second chance to be saved after death, nor the emptying and abolishing of hell. The reason I know what they do not mean is that these doctrines are simply not taught in the whole sweep of revealed truth. And more significantly, the exact opposite is fully and freely taught throughout the entire Bible.

I have used one passage of Scripture, not to emphasize it in particular, but as a fair example chosen from a dozen or so difficult passages found in the Bible. The same rule applies to each and all of them. The moral is: Let the whole Bible speak and you will find that it speaks with one clear voice. Listen to that voice and the obscure verses will not trouble you.

"He that hath ears to hear, let him hear" (Matthew 11:15). The wise will understand, but we may expect a certain type of religionist to continue to major on obscurities. He has a built-in talent for going askew on doctrine, and nothing I can say will cure him.

No Substitutes Accepted

Everything has its proper cause—in the kingdom of God as well as in the natural world. The reason for God's obvious refusal to send revival may lie deep, but surely not too deep to discover. We need only be realistic and honest as we confront the undeniable fact. *I believe that our problem is that we have been trying to substitute praying for obeying, and it simply won't work.*

A church, for instance, follows its traditions without much thought for whether or not they are scriptural. Or it surrenders to pressure from public opinion and falls in with the popular trends that carry it far from the New Testament pattern. Then the leaders notice a lack of spiritual power among the people and become concerned about it. What to do? How can they achieve that revitalization of spirit they need so badly? How can they bring down refreshing showers to quicken their fainting souls?

The answer is all ready for them. The books tell them how—pray! The passing evangelist confirms what the books have said—pray! The word is echoed back and forth, growing in volume until it becomes a roar—pray! So the pastor calls his people to prayer. Days and nights are spent begging God to be merciful and send revival upon His people. The tide of feeling runs high and it looks for a while as if the revival might be on its way. But nothing happens, and the zeal for prayer begins to flag. Before long the church is back where it was before and a numb discouragement settles over everyone. What has gone wrong?

Simply this—neither the leaders nor the people have made any effort to obey the Word of God. They felt that their only weakness was failure to pray, when actually in a score of ways they were falling short in vital matters of obedience. "To obey is better than sacrifice" (1 Samuel 15:22). Prayer is never an acceptable substitute for obedience. The sovereign Lord accepts no offering from His creatures that is not accompanied by obedience. To pray for revival while ignoring or actually flouting the plain precept laid down in the Scriptures is to waste a lot of words.

It has been quite overlooked in recent times that the faith of Christ is an absolute arbiter. It preempts the whole redeemed personality and seizes upon the individual to the exclusion of all other claims. Or, more accurately, it makes every legitimate claim on the Christian's life and without hesitation decides the place each claim shall have in the total scheme. The act of committal to Christ in salvation releases the believing man or woman from the penalty of sin, but it does not release him or her from the obligation to obey the words of Christ. Rather it brings that person under the joyous necessity to obey.

Many people think that the New Testament epistles are largely concerned with exhortation— merely good advice. By dividing the epistles into "doctrinal" and "exhortative" sections we have relieved ourselves of any necessity to obey. The doctrinal passages require nothing from us except that we believe them. The so-called exhortative passages are harmless enough, for the word by which they are described declares them to be words of advice and encouragement rather than commandments to be obeyed. This is a palpable error. *There is no advice in the New Testament* except three passages in the seventh chapter of Paul's first epistle to the Corinthians, and these are clearly marked as not bearing the credentials of divine inspiration (verses 6, 12, 25).

Apart from these, the "exhortations" in the epistles are to be understood as apostolic injunctions carrying the weight of mandatory charges from the Head of the church. They are intended to be obeyed, not weighed as bits of good advice that we are at liberty to accept or reject as we will.

If we would have God's blessing upon us we must begin to obey. Prayer will become effective when we stop using it as a substitute for obedience. We only deceive ourselves when we try to make the substitution.

Flee from Idolatry

Idolatry is of all sins the most hateful to God because it is in essence a defamation of the divine character. It holds a low opinion of God, and when it advertises that opinion, it is guilty of circulating an evil rumor about the Majesty in the heavens. Thus it slanders the Deity. No wonder God hates it.

We should beware of the comfortable habit of assuming that idolatry is found only in heathen lands and that civilized people are free from it. This is an error and results from pride and superficial thinking. The truth is that idolatry is found wherever mankind is found. Whoever entertains an unworthy conception of God is throwing his or her heart wide open to the sin of idolatry. Let that person go on to personalize his or her low mental image of the Deity and pray to it, and he or she has become an idolater—and this is regardless of his or her nominal profession of Christianity.

It is vitally important that we think soundly about God. Since He is the foundation of all our religious beliefs, it follows that if we err in our ideas of God, we will go astray on everything else.

The false gods of mankind have been and are many—almost as many as the worshipers themselves. It would require a good-size book just to list the gods that have received a name and been worshiped at sometime somewhere in the world. For sheer depravity the obscene phallic gods of the ancients were probably the lowest. Near to them and not far up on the scale came the scarab, the serpent, the bull and a whole menagerie of birds, four-footed beasts and creeping things. Paul says plainly that such degraded worship sprang from vain imaginations and darkened hearts resulting from the rejection of the knowledge of God.

Higher up the ladder came the nobler gods of the high-thinking philosophers and religionists of Greece, Persia and India. These represented the finest thinking about God by serious truth-seekers, but they fell short of the true God because they originated in the minds of fallen men and did not have the advantage of God's self-revelation to purify and correct their concepts. Their worship was and is idolatry.

It would be consoling to believe that such error is a thing of the past, that it belongs to the childhood of the race and to times and places long ago and far removed. But I wonder whether we would be justified in such a conclusion.

Where shall we classify the many current gods? What about the glorified chairman of the board of the American businessman? Or the storytelling, backslapping god of some of the service clubs? Or the broad-shouldered, ruddy-faced god who hears the prayers of pugilists bent on mayhem and money? Then there is the dreamy-eyed god of the unregenerate poet. This god is cozy and aesthetic and likes to fellowship with anybody who thinks high thoughts and believes in social equality.

Two other modern gods might be mentioned, different from each other in character and yet much alike in that they are both false gods. One is the tricky, unscrupulous god of the superstitious. He is the god of the chain-letter brigade and of all those who practice white magic. Though he is a cheap, class-D god, he still has many devotees in the United States. The other is the unwieldy, brain-heavy god of the unconverted theologian. He is known only to the intellectually elite, shows marked partiality to the learned and hobnobs exclusively with men possessing many degrees.

The Scriptures are the only trustworthy revelation of God, and we depart from them at our own peril. Nature tells us something about Him but not enough to save us from drawing erroneous conclusions about Him. What we can learn from nature must be completed and corrected by the Scriptures if we would escape wrong and unworthy concepts of God.

The heavens declare Thy glory, Lord!
In every star Thy wisdom shines;

But when our eyes behold Thy Word,
We read Thy name in fairer lines.

Of course the final revelation of God is Christ. "He that hath seen me hath seen the Father" (John 14:9). "Who being the brightness of his glory, and the express image of his person" (Hebrews 1:3). To know and follow Christ is to be saved from all forms of idolatry.

CHAPTER

39

Human Self-Sufficiency Is a Myth

Only God is self-sufficient. When men boast of being self-sufficient, they are indulging a fiction that can be proven fictitious just by taking a quick look around.

Wherever there is life there is constant expenditure of energy and the need for continual renewal to keep the organism going. To sustain life, a right balance must be maintained between the outgo and the intake of energy. When an organism is forced to expend more energy than it can create, and this is continued past a certain point, life ceases and the whole structure falls apart. We call that condition death.

This elementary law of life is taken for granted by the human race, and provision is made within the social framework for the intake of matter from which the body can create energy to replace that lost in normal activity. This matter we call food, and we refer to its reception into the organism as eating. The whole thing is an accepted phenomenon of human life, so we tend to overlook the profound lesson it teaches—*no living thing is self-sufficient.*

The human body cannot live on itself. To live it must have constant help from the outside. Though filled with pride and overflowing with self-assurance, men must humble themselves to receive aid from the lower creation. Every monarch must trust the common cow for food. Every strutting lord of the manor must beg his dinner from the barnyard hen. The cold prima donna manages to stay alive only by the grace of pigs and fish. The genius must look to bees, shrubs, seeds and berries. From these things come the energy without which all men would die, the great as well as the lowly.

In one sense everyone lives by faith. There is a kind of natural faith necessary before we sit down to eat. Those who scorn faith must nevertheless exercise it or they cannot continue to receive food. And whatever they may say, they *do* exercise it. They eat regular meals in complete confidence that the hens, cows, grain and bees will not let them down. Their trust is well justified, their food nourishes their body; life and energy reward their faith.

What men forget is that the body is just the dwelling place of the soul and, as the great Commoner so eloquently said, the soul is "a royal guest come to dwell for a while in a tenement house of clay." What is taught by prophet and apostle, as well as by Christ Himself, is that the soul is not self-sufficient.

It cannot live on itself. For life it must look to something, someone outside its own organism.

This deep need of the soul for life-giving bread is met fully in the person of our Lord Jesus Christ. "My Father giveth you the true bread from heaven" (John 6:32). He told the listeners and went on to identify that bread with Himself. "I am the bread of life: he that cometh to me shall never hunger; and he that believeth on me shall never thirst" (6:35). With only the most elementary knowledge of how things live by taking the material of life into them from outside, we should be able to understand the text, "The just shall live by faith" (Galatians 3:11).

Though the natural faith by which men live the natural life is entirely different from saving faith, it nevertheless illustrates saving faith, and reveals by analogy how it operates. The humble person receives Christ into him or herself by trustfully partaking. What eating is to the body, believing is to the soul. To gaze with the eyes of the heart is to believe. "No man is justified by the law in the sight of God, it is evident: for, The just shall live by faith" (3:11). So we are saved by believing, and we are saved by looking because looking and believing are the same.

The tragic history of the world is, at the bottom line, the record of sinning men trying to live on their own resources and never succeeding, because they are ignoring the most simple law of creation—*no living thing is self-sufficient*. God made us dependent upon Him. Either we recognize our need of Him, or we adopt the false philosophy of independence and go on our stubborn way to die at last and everlastingly.

CHAPTER

40

Why We Can
Never Escape Problems

Wherever two surfaces moving in different directions touch each other, there is friction, and wherever there is friction there is heat. In the operation of our highly complex modern machinery, friction is a serious problem. The resistance one moving part offers to another can slow down all motion and bring the machine to a halt, or the heat generated by one surface moving over another can burn up the whole thing. To prevent this, all contact surfaces are made as smooth as possible, and lubricants are used between the parts to reduce the friction to a minimum. Without lubricating oil the industries of a modern nation would grind to a full stop within a few minutes.

A machine is a society of metal parts, so to speak, each part having its own work to do toward the fulfillment of the purpose for which the machine was designed. Opposing parts may give the impression of working against each other, but actually they are working together toward an end too high to be achieved by any individual part working alone—an end which can only be realized by the efforts of the whole society.

The parts of a machine serve as an allegory of human society. A man standing alone is just a man, but as soon as another man walks up and joins him, we have a society of men. Because two men cannot stand still or be silent for long, this elementary society soon develops social problems. The separate interests of the two men cause them to move in different directions, and because they are in contact there will be friction. Now, instead of that simple society of two men, think of a full-blown society of men, women and children, and it is easy to see why the world has troubles. If humanity stood still, or if all its members were alike and had identical interests, there would be no problems in human society. The energy and activity of men, however, make a certain amount of friction inevitable.

From this we Christians may learn much. Because the church is a society of human beings, the problems that plague families and nations are found in the church, too. If a Christian stands by himself, his only problems are personal, but as soon as other Christians join him, he has social problems as well. True, the members of the church are *redeemed* human beings, but that fact does not make them any less human. Differences of taste, temperament, opinion, moral energy and speed of action among religious people in close association create a certain amount of friction in the group. Wise Christian leaders will anticipate this and will know what to do when it develops.

This is written for the consolation of God's people, especially ministers and Christian workers. If we come to the practical business of living in the local Christian community with unrealistic notions concerning it, we are in for a bitter disillusionment and perhaps some soul injuries that will not heal.

When I was a young preacher with my first tiny pastorate, I had not had enough experience to know what to expect. I came to the work of the church with the naive belief that the twin wonders of the new birth and the indwelling of the Spirit would make discord and unpleasantness among the saints impossible. Consequently, the first flare-up in the church nearly crushed my spirit. Unconsciously I had thought that I had been called to shepherd a flock of angels instead of a flock of human sheep. Through agonizing prayer and deep suffering, I finally came to see what I should have known in the first place—that Christians are basically human beings, and when they try to live together, they will have problems just like other people. The church is a body of moving parts, a society of many members. The problems arising in any church will be in direct proportion to the zeal, the activity and the energy of its members. This is inevitable and should be taken in stride.

Some misguided Christian leaders feel that they must preserve harmony at any cost, so they do everything possible to reduce friction. They should remember that there is no friction in a machine that has been shut down for the night. Turn off the power, and you will have no problem with moving parts. Also remember that there is a human society where there are no problems—the cemetery. The dead have no differences of opinion. They generate no heat, because they have no energy and no motion. But their penalty is sterility and complete lack of achievement.

What then is the conclusion of the matter? That problems are the price of progress, that friction is the concomitant of motion, that a live and expanding church will have a certain quota of difficulties as a result of its life and activity. A Spirit-filled church will invite the anger of the enemy.

How then shall we deal with our problems? First, expect them so you will not be taken off guard. Second, realize that every live body of Christians has it troubles, from Christ and His apostles to the present day, so yours are not unique. Third, pour in copious amounts of love, the best lubricant in the world. Love will reduce friction to a minimum and keep the whole body working smoothly and without injury to its parts. Where does this love come from? The love of God bursts forth from the Holy Spirit in our hearts.

The Captain of Souls

The English poet, William Ernest Henley, has had a world of abuse heaped upon him by some indignant Christians who bitterly resent his having said in plain words what practically everyone believes:

> I am the master of my fate:
> I am the captain of my soul.

Although the prevailing tone of the poem is arrogant and defiant in a frightened sort of way, I think we would do well to be charitable toward its author, a man whose heart knew nothing of the softening influences of the love of God, a lifelong cripple who was moved to strike out blindly at whatever it was that, as he saw it, gave him such an unfair deal. His ill-humored bugling at the heavens above has more than a trace of bravado and wishful thinking. And yet his lines about being the captain of his soul and the master of his fate are true.

Charles Wesley said much the same thing in a hymn that has been sung by virtually every church in the English-speaking world:

> A charge to keep I have,
>
>   A God to glorify;
> A never-dying soul to save
>   And fit it for the sky.

Only those who deny the freedom of the human will could object to Wesley's lines. Certainly God has given each of us a soul, and just as certainly He has charged us to see that it is saved. Peter's words to the multitudes at Pentecost convey this idea: "Save yourselves from this untoward generation" (Acts 2:40). Who can doubt that Peter conceived his hearers to be responsible for their own spiritual condition? To think otherwise is to read into his words meaning that is surely not there.

Waiving for a moment the technical distinction between the captain and the pilot of a ship, we can see how each man is the captain of his own soul. As soon as the ship has slipped her mooring and is out on the bosom of the deep, the captain alone is responsible for her. The whole expanse of the seven seas is before her. "Behold also the ships, which though they be so great, and are driven of fierce winds, yet are they turned about with a very small helm, whithersoever the governor listeth" (James 3:4).

But we do not like to think that we are responsible for our own souls. It is a disconcerting, even terrifying thought. We are so weak, so ignorant, and the sea is so vast and cruel. "Lord, we know not whither thou goest; and how can we know the way?" (John 14:5) Thomas exclaimed, and in so doing gave expression to our own feelings. We don't even know where the harbor is—how can we hope to reach it? And yet we are responsible—how can these things be?

The answer is that while we cannot pilot our ship safely into the harbor ourselves, *we can choose to put our vessel into the hands of One who can.* God has given us our free will in order that we may choose the right pilot. He has also provided the Pilot, Jesus Christ our Lord. We only need to acknowledge our own ignorance and cry out in faith,

> Jesus, Saviour, pilot me
> Over life's tempestuous sea;
> Unknown waves before me roll,
> Hiding rock and treacherous shoal;
> Chart and compass come from Thee:
> Jesus, Saviour, pilot me.

God has given each one a will of his own. The difference between a Christian and an unsaved person is not that one has a will and the other does not. No, both have wills. *The difference is what they do with them.* The sinner wills to run his or her own life, and that is the essence of sin. Christians are Christians because in faith they surrendered their will to the will of God and turned their soul over to Jesus Christ. Tennyson understood this when he wrote,

> Our wills are ours, we know not how;
> Our wills are ours, to make them Thine.

The conclusion of the matter is that the fate of every man has a master and the soul of every man has a captain. It is either the man himself or Another whom he has chosen. The difference can be stated in a few words, but the mighty eternal outworkings of it could not be written in a thousand books. Heaven and hell, life and death, happiness and woe hang upon the decision—Christ or me? Poor Henley. He was so right, yet so frightfully, tragically wrong.

What Is the "Deeper Life"?

I t is becoming more evident every day that there has occurred in the United States over the past few years a positive movement toward a higher type of Christian life. Just when the various "holiness" churches have been reduced to virtual impotence and the bulk of fundamentalism has sold its birthright for a mess of pottage, a counter movement has arisen within the body of contemporary Christian believers. Apparently this movement did not originate with any one man or woman or in any one place. Rather it is a spontaneous upspringing of spiritual desire among Christians of many and varying religious backgrounds. The movement is not organized—it has no local headquarters, no officers and no dues-paying members. So silently and mysteriously has its influence permeated modern evangelicalism that it can be likened to the action of the wind that "blows wherever it pleases" without earthly agency or previous human knowledge. Though the movement has no new doctrine or peculiar ideas, its members recognize each other wherever they meet and reach across denominational lines to clasp warm hands and whisper, "Brother!" "Sister!"

The growing interest in the deeper life on the part of rapidly increasing numbers of religious people is significant. The term itself is not new nor is it the property of any particular group or school of interpretation. The words, or something like them, have been used at various times in church history to identify a revolt against the ordinary in Christian experience and the insatiable yearning of a few discontented souls after the deep, essentially spiritual and inward power of the Christian message.

The fact that so many professed Christians should be concerned with a "deeper life" is tacit evidence that their spiritual experience has not been satisfactory. Many have looked themselves over and have turned away disappointed. When they talked to other professed Christians, they discovered that others were no better off than themselves. Surely, they reasoned hopefully, there must be something better, sweeter, deeper than what they were experiencing day by day. So they have turned eagerly to the advocates of the deeper life and inquired earnestly, if a bit cautiously, just what they are talking about and where it is found in Holy Scriptures.

The deeper life must be understood to mean a life in the Spirit far in advance of the average and nearer to the New Testament norm. I do not know that the term is the best that could be chosen, but for want of a better one we shall continue to employ it. There are many scriptural phrases that embody the meaning we are attempting to convey, but *these have been interpreted downward and equated with the spiritual mediocrity now current. The consequence is that when they are used by the average Bible teacher today, they do not mean what they meant when they were first used by the inspired writers.* This is the penalty we pay for making the Word of God conform to our experience instead of bringing our experience up to the Word of God. When high scriptural terms are used to describe low spiritual living, then other and more definitive terms are needed. Only by using terms previously agreed upon and understood can there be true communication between teacher and learner. Hence this definition of the deeper life.

The deeper life has also been called the "victorious life," but I do not like that term. It appears to me that it focuses attention exclusively upon one feature of the Christian life, that of personal victory over sin, when actually this is just one aspect of the deeper life—an important one, to be sure, but only one. That life in the Spirit that is denoted by the term "deeper life" is far wider and richer than mere victory over sin, however vital that victory may be. It also includes the thought of the indwelling of Christ, acute God-consciousness, rapturous worship, separation from the world, the joyous surrender of everything to God, internal union with the Trinity, the practice of the presence of God, the communion of saints and prayer without ceasing.

To enter upon such a life, seekers must be ready to accept without question the New Testament as the one final authority on spiritual matters. They must be willing to make Christ the one supreme Lord and ruler in their lives. They must surrender their whole being to the destructive power of the cross, to die not only to their sins but to their righteousness as well as to everything in which they formerly prided themselves.

If this should seem like a heavy sacrifice for anyone to make, let it be remembered that Christ is Lord and can make any demands upon us that He chooses, even to the point of requiring that we deny ourselves and bear the cross daily. The mighty anointing of the Holy Spirit that follows will restore to the soul infinitely more than has been taken away. It is a hard way, but a glorious one. Those who have known the sweetness of it will never complain about what they have lost. They will be too well pleased with what they have gained.

Titles by A.W. Tozer available
through your local Christian bookstore:

The Attributes of God
The Attributes of God Journal
The Best of A.W. Tozer (two volumes)
Born after Midnight
The Christian Book of Mystical Verse
Christ the Eternal Son
The Counselor
The Early Tozer: A Word in Season
Echoes from Eden
Faith Beyond Reason
Gems from Tozer
God Tells the Man Who Cares
How to Be Filled with the Holy Spirit
I Call It Heresy!
I Talk Back to the Devil
Jesus, Author of Our Faith
Jesus Is Victor!
Jesus, Our Man in Glory
Let My People Go, A biography of Robert A. Jaffray
Man: The Dwelling Place of God
Men Who Met God
The Next Chapter after the Last
Of God and Men
Paths to Power
The Price of Neglect
The Pursuit of God
The Pursuit of Man (formerly *The Divine Conquest*)
The Quotable Tozer
The Quotable Tozer II
Renewed Day by Day, Vol. 1
Renewed Day by Day, Vol. 2
The Root of the Righteous
Rut, Rot or Revival
The Set of the Sail